Own It!

How Great Leaders Build a
'Take Responsibility' Culture
for Breakthrough Results

Chris J. Ihrig

Fired Up Publishing, Inc.
Puyallup, WA

This edition published by Fired Up Publishing, a division of Fired Up Brands, Inc. For information address Fired Up Brands, Puyallup, WA.

First Edition
ISBN 978-1-7366624-4-1
Cataloging-in-Publication Data

Ihrig, Chris J., 1967-
Own It! How Great Leaders Build a 'Take Responsibility' Culture for Breakthrough Results. / Chris J. Ihrig p. cm.

Includes bibliographical references and index.

Summary: ""Describes how business leaders can create an Own It Culture by changing the social contract between management and employees, encouraging emergent leaders, and delivering customer value to drive breakthrough business results."--Provided by publisher.

ISBN 978-1-7366624-4-1 (pbk. : alk. paper)
1. Leadership. 2. Organizational behavior. 3. Organizational effectiveness. 4. Management--Employee participation. 5. Responsibility. 6. Self-management 7. Workplace Culture.

Editing and Proofing by Matthew Ralph
Exterior cover design by Vanessa Mendozzi
Interior book design by Probookdesigns

Manufactured in the United States of America

To my wonderful wife and children.

The journey of life is one of ups and downs, unexpected curves, tears and joy. No matter what shows up at the doorstep, I have come to a place of great appreciation that I get to do this thing called life with each of you. I have grown because of you. I have found the strength to be vulnerable and courageous because of you. It is with all my heart that I thank you for your unconditional love for me. Without each of you and the journey we have been on, neither this book nor my work would have happened.

I love you.
Chris

TABLE OF CONTENTS

INTRODUCTION

"I alone cannot change the world, but I can cast a stone across the water to create many ripples."
- Mother Teresa

My name is Chris Ihrig and I'm CEO and Founder of Fired Up Culture, a leadership coaching and workplace culture consulting firm. My work has taken me and my team around the globe and afforded us the opportunity to partner with leaders who are guiding diverse organizations. Some of these organizations are small and local, while others are large and global. Whether a not-for-profit or a publicly held company, one thing is true: leadership matters. Our team has made it our mission to work alongside leaders, equip them to become champions of workplace culture, and be the change agents our world needs.

For the past several decades of my own professional journey as an Executive Coach and Organizational Change Agent, I've studied the business models of the successful and those that fail. Even with all the variables that exist and the complexities that are inherent in the business environment, a constant truth remains:

Handing over the reins of authority to team members turns out to be a good business strategy.

When controls are relaxed, that is, when team members are given the freedom to do what they want, the outcomes are typically a resounding success. For organizations that fail, the pattern is the opposite. We find that when controls are increased, results decline.

The best organizations in the world expect their people to take responsibility for their jobs, to continually improve the systems they work with, and most importantly, to deliver customer value. While the leaders of these organizations have high expectations of their people, they give people the freedom to take responsibility for their work, without resulting to 'command-and-control' tactics, or worse, bullying behaviors.

These bold leaders expect workers to measure and monitor their own results, and to be directly accountable to their customers, to their co-workers, and to the organization. Their philosophy about people is: "People really want to be great – and if they're not great, it's because the culture we've created won't let them be great."

It was from this place that our consulting firm, Fired Up Culture, and the frameworks for our work was born. And whether we're working with a not-for-profit or a publicly held entity, whether there are 20 team members or an army of thousands, the philosophy and practice of building a take responsibility or "Own It Culture" is the difference maker.

I've found that contrary to what many CEOs assume, leadership is not really about delegating tasks and monitoring results; it's about infusing the entire workforce with a sense of responsibility for the business.[1] In other words, the most successful organizations create cultures where people *own* the work.

You may think this philosophy - "people really want to be great" - reflects a certain naivety about human nature. I do admit that we live in a world where people often disappoint us. I also acknowledge that ego and the relentless pursuit of self-interest often bring out the worst in us.

If we're smarter, more talented, or more powerful than those around us, we may give in to the temptation of taking advantage of those less gifted or powerful than ourselves. I also recognize that when we feel threatened, we often do whatever it takes to survive, even if it harms us or our organizations.

I also admit that sometimes we're just plain selfish and lazy; it's easier to take care of ourselves and our own needs, rather than worry about taking responsibility for serving the needs of others.

Organizations often give in to the pressures of growth. This is a workplace culture issue that many organizations struggle to navigate when the challenges of growth or other pressure moments hit. This remains true whether it's a "mom and pop shop" that is doubling the workforce, or even a large global business moving through a complex change process with thousands of dispersed teams.

How quickly and successfully organizations, and the people that make up the workforce, navigate these challenging times will depend on whether they embrace and unleash three strategies which I describe in this book:

In Part I, *Changing the Social Contract.* I discuss how to change a social contract that inhibits responsibility-taking, and I explain how to build a foundation for a new, healthier social contract based on *Connected Values.*

In Part II, *Building an Own It Culture.* I introduce the actions that *Emergent Leaders* should be encouraged to do that will assist their colleagues to take responsibility for assuming ownership of their jobs and for finding innovative ways of improving the systems they work with.

In Part III, *Delivering on the Customer Promise.* I show how to link responsibility and accountability, so that self-managing functional teams, and cross-functional teams called *TransFormation Zones,* can consistently deliver customer value.

Throughout this book, I reference companies as models of proficiency who have suffered at times as a result of forgetting these three key strategies.

Some examples include Nordstrom, which lost its way when prompting Bruce Nordstrom to the helm of the organization to repair the company's then-flagging reputation. Harley-Davidson had its problems maintaining good communication and relations with its workers, which lead to a strike. Patagonia too admits to mistakes.

The point is: no company, even those that I cite as those who "get it", are immune from forgetting what earned them their success in the first place. My team and I, on a regular basis, witness organizations that have lost their way by diverting away from these principles.

Yet even though individuals and companies behave selfishly at times, I believe human beings also have an enormous capacity to behave with selflessness. Despite the dark side of our human nature, most of us come to eventually realize that life is not simply about achieving our own self-interests. We understand that life is richer by far when we take responsibility for living a life of service to others.

How do courageous leaders take responsibility for choosing selflessness over self-interest? To begin with, these responsible leaders don't waste their time trying to change the behavior of individuals who are unable or unwilling to choose to take responsibility. Instead, these heroic leaders establish a healthy work environment where people from the top to the bottom are motivated to behave responsibly.

Edwin H. Friedman, the man who pioneered the application of family theory to religious, medical, education, business, and governmental institutions, argues that trying to change the behavior of unmotivated people is a waste of time.

As Friedman puts it: "They cannot learn from experience, which is why the unmotivated are invulnerable to insight."

No amount of understanding or empathy will cause unmotivated people to mature or make them responsible, says Friedman. They're the least mature, the most disruptive, and tend to be the chronic troublemakers. They're highly reactive to events, and also reactive to one another. They place the blame for their own troubles on others – especially management. They see themselves as victims, refusing to take responsibility for their own choices.

Friedman summarizes: "There are forces on this planet that, because of their inability or unwillingness to self-regulate, are by nature all take and no give."[2]

Therefore, the wise leader focuses their energy and attention on the people who can and will take responsibility. Once a "Own It Culture" is established, most of the unwilling choose to leave; and those who don't are eventually asked to leave. Certainly, responsibility-resistant people are given the chance to adjust their behaviors and attitudes (as I describe in Part I of this book) to choose to become responsible. But in the end, people must choose for themselves.

In today's fast-paced, highly competitive world, is it possible to get people to 'own it' when a growing number of organizations and individuals are avoiding responsibility? The evidence I will present in this book shows that the answer is a resounding YES!

Organizations where people are encouraged to manage themselves and to take responsibility for their own jobs, the systems they work with and stay focused on delivering customer value, significantly outperform the conventional cultures where bosses impose control.

When the bald eagle population was threatened, America took action to improve the environment so that their numbers could recover, and they could once again thrive – and we've succeeded.

In the same way, organizations that want to survive and succeed in a challenging world must create an "Own It Culture" where Emergent Leaders take responsibility for delivering customer value is commonplace. An environment where every member of the organization is free to soar like a superhero.

SECTION 1:

CHANGING THE SOCIAL CONTRACT

*"It is easier to fight for one's principles
than to live up to them."*
– Alfred Adler

In this Section:

- Challenging the Social Contract
- Building a Foundation of Values
- Reducing the Values Gap
- Increasing Team Member Engagement
- Tapping into Intrinsic Motivation
- Eliminating Toxic Behaviors
- Rising Above Learned Helplessness

O ne of my personal life passions is playing golf. I love the challenge, but I also really enjoy the opportunity to be outside in the rhythm of play where my mind can decompress from the challenges of our world, all while hitting a little white ball.

No matter where around the globe I find myself playing 18 holes, it's a fantastic chance to meet people. Well, let me be more descriptive. It's a chance to be introduced to a wide variety of people that make up our human race. Some are salty characters who carry with them a very poor attitude about life. Others are people who are truly out for the joy of the experience and carry a triumphant attitude no matter what happens.

So, why am I choosing to start this book by talking about golf? It was during a particular round several summers back when I experienced a life changing 'Aha' moment. That moment led to a deeper dedication to my work and frankly the thoughts and frameworks you're about to receive in this book. This particular round truly was about personal transformation that has led to me 'owning it'.

On a particular day in late summer, I had ventured out to a course close to my home in Washington state, called Chambers Bay. It's become one of my favorite places to play. It's challenging, but breathtaking. I was so looking forward to getting outside and playing some golf.

The week before had been a difficult week at work. I was trying to do my best to lead a team in a work environment that had many challenges. I was struggling to understand what was going on, why my team was struggling, and why the results were simply not being achieved. It had been this way for several years and it was just then that I had reached a point of fatigue, frustration and legitimate resolution that this is what work was always going to be about.

I wanted to be a good leader, but I was really confused and lost as to how to do it well. During our round of golf, I shared some of my leadership struggles.

The gentleman I was assigned to play golf with on this day was Joe. It didn't take him long to realize I was having some work struggles. He was a curious chap who seemed to really care about what was going on. I shared a few things with him. Later in our game, he shared the story of his first job in college: being a "helper" for a contractor.

This is the story, Joe shared with me:

"On my first day, the foreman handed me a shovel and told me to dig a 30-foot long, two-foot-deep trench in the rock-hard clay soil. The Forman sternly stated, 'You better not foul it up ... rookie.' Little did I know that digging the trench was a test to see if the 'new kid' was tough enough to work alongside seasoned construction workers.

"Being the rookie on the crew, I was treated like a slave. I was regularly sworn at, threatened, blamed for screw-ups, and otherwise verbally abused on a daily basis. I learned to keep my mouth shut and do what I was told. While I was not the only man on the job who was on the receiving the daily abuse, I noticed how others were coping. The crew would deliberately slow down their pace of work, they'd complain endlessly about the boss, and it wasn't unusual for someone to quit work without warning."

As I listened, a light bulb went on. As the moment of clarity became even more intense, a question formed in my mind: "What's leadership got to do with this?"

Too often, we find ourselves working for bosses who act like bullies, and with co-workers who are discouraged, unmotivated, or even destructive. As I continued to process Joe's story and my frustrations for the week, I came to realize that these behaviors are not usually a result of having hired the wrong people (which, of course, is always a possibility). Instead, these behaviors are a predictable result of normal human beings trapped in a toxic work environment.

Put simply:

Toxic organizational cultures bring out the worst in people.

CHAPTER 1

The Good, The Bad and The Ugly of Workplace Culture

"

The past cannot be changed. The future is yet in your power."
– Unknown

Over my years of working with diverse organizations around the world, I've come to recognize there are many types of Workplace Cultures. Some are thriving, others struggle a great deal. As part of most of our client engagements, we do some culture assessment work. Essentially, we gather the thoughts and opinions of the team members of the organization. I like to call it "getting the voice of the people to the table." Through this assessment work, I have the opportunity to get into the hearts and minds of the people working in these places.

As workers share individual stories and experiences, it's clear the frustrations and joys they feel are wide and varied. The experience of work is not the same for everyone. Through my coaching conversations with hundreds, if not thousands, of professionals, it's evident that there is a good, bad and ugly side of workplace culture.

As part of my professional journey, I've been on a quest to discover what were the factors that caused someone to experience a wonderful, engaging and life-giving workplace versus one that sucked the soul out of the person.

The answers always came back to the issue of leadership and how effective they were at building, investing and sustaining solid relationships while balancing that with the need to drive results. Consistent in all this research, leaders were able to masterfully put together the right set of tools and apply them affectively that ultimately unleashes a 'take responsibility' or, as I call it, an "Own It" attitude and set of behaviors in the people they're leading.

It starts with the ownership of the Social Contracts that exists in the workplace culture.

Challenging the Social Contract

Thomas Hobbes, the first modern philosopher to articulate a detailed social contract theory, said that people allow others to rule over them in return for their protection. This is the social contract that most workers enter into when they accept a job: they agree to do what those in authority tell them to do and in exchange, they receive wages and some measure of job security.

Every group of people who live and/or work together learn to get along by observing the often unwritten, and commonly understood, 'social contract'. A social contract tells people what to expect of one another, what roles they play, and how to be successful in the group.

Elementary school kids observe a social contract that tells them where they fit in on the playground. The strong and the quick kids rule over the weak and the slow. In a college fraternity, the senior students rule over the pledges. Those who rule either by intimidation or subtle manipulation fight hard to preserve the status quo.

To those in positions of authority, telling others what to do and how to do it may seem perfectly appropriate – especially if the people under their authority seem to be unable or unwilling to take responsibility. But why is it that people who are able to function as responsible adults off the job, such as by raising a family, participating in community-building activities, and paying their taxes, fail to behave responsibly on the job?

I would suggest that this happens because these people are simply conforming to a social contract that really doesn't expect them to behave responsibly. What's even more unfortunate is that when people in a conventional work environment are finally given a small amount of authority, they often show symptoms of what I call "The Deputy Fife Syndrome."

The Deputy Fife Syndrome

Ok, you might be falling into one of two categories right now. Those of you who know who Deputy Fife is and those who have no clue. It really doesn't matter. What does matter is that we understand what the Deputy Fife Syndrome is and how it ultimately impacts our relationships in the workplace.

If you've ever watched "classic television" you know that Barney Fife was the hyperkinetic and comically inept deputy sheriff played by the late Don Knotts on the 1960s television series, *The Andy Griffith Show.* It was Barney's ham-handed approach to exercising his power and authority as a deputy sheriff that often got him into trouble. The syndrome describes symptoms and behaviors of those who assert control or authority in an inappropriate or destructive manner – as in a bully.

Undoubtedly, you've seen people in the workplace who behave like Deputy Fife: the co-worker who, when put in charge of a meeting, shuts down any ideas other than their own. Perhaps it's the newly promoted frontline supervisor who issues orders to their former co-workers like a drill sergeant, or the middle-manager who micro-manages everything.

As a customer, you've also no doubt experienced people who display symptoms of the Deputy Fife Syndrome: the technical support person who refuses to help you resolve a problem in simple language, the retail clerk who talks in a patronizing tone while explaining that you can't return the purchase without a receipt, or the hostess who refuses to seat you ten minutes before your reservation even though the table is open.

The justification often given by these bullies is that they are "just following the rules" (of the social contract).

Don't misunderstand this. The rules of the social contract are useful in that they give us the boundaries that we can be successful in. Rules keep us from harm. Rules provide structure which a society or an organization can function and thrive on.

While rules help us get along with our neighbors and resolve our disputes, the rules can also get in the way, and in the hands of someone behaving like Deputy Fife, can be used as weapons. Deputy Fife's problem was that he enforced the rules at the wrong times and for the wrong reasons. Rules were a vehicle for asserting his limited authority over others, and in doing so, protecting his fragile self-esteem.

For someone susceptible to the Deputy Fife Syndrome, being given a small amount of power and authority can be like taking a powerful drug. Having felt powerless in the past or having been victimized by their abusive bosses, the Deputy Fifes of the world are likely to exercise their newfound authority with great zeal, but often without compassion or wisdom.

When given the opportunity to exercise even a small measure of authority, a worker who has been abused by other Deputy Fifes may also become a bully.

Managers and supervisors showing symptoms of The Deputy Fife Syndrome may justify their bullying behavior by rationalizing that the people working for them can't be trusted. They base this on their experience that the more they assert their authority, the more the people who report to them resist and disappoint them.

Like Deputy Fife, they may see themselves as morally superior. They never stop to think that their authoritarian application of power might be the cause of responsibility inhibiting behaviors and poor performance. They prefer to believe that people are lazy or incompetent. When the pressure is really on, Deputy Fifes have a tendency to try to bring order out of chaos by bullying the people under them into compliance.

One of the underlying reasons why people in a position of authority behave like bullies is what Dr. Carol Dweck calls a "fixed mindset."

"The fixed mindset creates an urgency to prove yourself over and over," says Dr. Dweck. "If you have only a certain amount of intelligence, a certain personality, and a certain moral character — well, then, you'd better prove that you have a healthy dose of them."[3]

In other words, people with a fixed mindset tend to believe that their talents and abilities are set in stone, so they try to look smart and talented at all costs. They avoid anything that might make them look stupid or incompetent and employ tactics to shift the blame for their failures onto others. What often looks like a display of excessive pride and arrogance often turns out to be a cover for underlying insecurity, low self-esteem, or even self-loathing.

Toxic Social Contracts

A more disturbing reason that people in positions of authority tend to bully others was brought out in the famous *Stanford Prison Experiment.* In the experiment, Philip Zimbardo and his colleagues at Stanford University divided a small group of college-student volunteers into inmates and guards and placed them into a simulated prison environment. The results of the experiment showed how quickly a toxic social contract can bring out the dark side of our human nature and cause people to behave in ways that are destructive.

The experiment originally designed to go on for a full week spiraled out of control in just four days. The guard's treatment of the prisoners had pushed a few of the prisoners to the brink of psychological break-down.

Zimbardo summed up the bullying behavior observed in the young men assigned to the role of guards this way: "Ordinary, normal, healthy young men succumbed to, or were seduced by, the social forces inherent in that behavioral context [having absolute power and control over the prisoners]... The line between good and evil, once thought to be impermeable, proved instead to be quite permeable."

In short, the behavior of the young men who were assigned as guards very quickly became brutal.

The social dynamics that turn good people into bullies is quite complex. Beside the factors already mentioned, they include the need to belong, the tendency for excessive conformity and compliance, a desire to be part of the "in group," and hostility toward the "out group." These common human needs "can be perverted into an excessive exercise of power to dominate others [by those placed in positions of authority] or learned helplessness [for those in positions of subservience]."[4]

The young men cast in the role of prisoners in the Stanford Prison Experiment quickly showed evidence of "learned helplessness" (we'll talk more about this term later in the book) as they were subjected to the dehumanizing effects of the guard's brutal tactics. In order to survive in a very hostile environment, these young men cast in the role of prisoners suppressed their normal emotions, identities, and moral compasses. Instead, they did whatever they felt they had to do in order to survive.

For many people in America and throughout the world, the social contract has created a work environment that is similar to a prison. Like the Stanford Prison Experiment, people in conventional top-down cultures are divided into two groups: managers (guards) and workers (prisoners) with very similar toxic behavioral results. The managers often become bullies — even if they don't behave that way elsewhere – and the workers become "difficult," often resorting to an array of responsibility avoiding behaviors.

Both the managers and the workers are doing their best to adapt and survive in a toxic social contract. It's not that these conventional organizations have somehow recruited and hired "bullies" as managers and "helpless" or "difficult" workers. It's quite the opposite: most of these organizations recruit normal, hard-working, well-intentioned human beings. But very quickly, a toxic social contract brings out the worst in people.

You've probably seen headlines like: Fund Manager Bilks Investors Out of Billions of Dollars; CEO of Major Company Convicted of Fraud; Government Official Found Guilty of Corruption.

How do these things happen? Are these "white-collar criminals" somehow different from the rest of us? Are they simply sociopaths who eventually get found out because they let their greed overcome their efforts to keep their crimes hidden? Perhaps. However, these lawbreakers are rarely able to commit these crimes without the help of co-workers who stay silent.

Their co-workers know, or at least suspect, that something wrong is going on, but choose not to confront the wrongdoing because they fear they might be either implicated or fired. And they have good reason to be afraid. Our society's whistle-blowers have often suffered greatly for having done the right thing.

Very slowly, by simply choosing to ignore wrongdoing, a new social contract evolves: one where toxic behavior become the group norm. Seeing that those in authority either ignore or condone toxic behavior, others either join in or simply look the other way.

While some members of the group might be bothered by what's going on, they're afraid to confront it. Unfortunately, this state of affairs is similar to the fable of boiling a frog. If you place a live frog in a pot of tepid water and slowly increase the temperature of the water, the frog doesn't notice the increasing temperature until it's too late. In the same way, people living under a social contract where toxic behavior is tolerated or ignored often find themselves in the pot with the other frogs.

On the other hand, an "Own It Culture" encourages people to challenge any behavior that threatens the health of the organization. They establish a high standard of honesty and integrity, which they protect vigorously; they encourage an open-mindset and have broken down the walls between management and labor by establishing a new social contract based on *Values*.

CHAPTER 2

Own It: Changing the Social Contract

"

A tiny change today brings a dramatically different tomorrow."
– Richard Bach

I n 1972, graduate students in the sociology department of a major university in the United States began a research project seeking a link between individual job satisfaction and an organizational success. Initially, they surveyed nearly 2.5 million workers and managers in the United States across 32 different industries.

No conclusive correlations or links were found. These graduate students then broadened their research to 40 countries. This expansion generated an additional 14.5 million survey responses, for a total of 17 million survey responses. Unfortunately for them, after almost three years of work, they found no conclusive statistical correlation between individual job satisfaction and organizational performance. Reluctantly, the graduate students and their faculty advisors abandoned their work, concluding that the data was of little or no value.

The survey data gathered dust in a dark corner of the university's dead files until 15 years later when a new study of the work was launched. This time, it deployed the research based on the methodology of John Naisbitt, a former Assistant Secretary of Education to President Kennedy. He used this methodology to write his bestseller, *Mega Trends*. By measuring and recording the total column inches in newspapers and magazines devoted to news stories, Naisbitt was able to predict, with surprising accuracy, any future social, political, spiritual and economic mega trends.

Using the same methodology, researchers looked for the words and phrases that occurred most often in the *comments* section at the end of the survey. With the help of a computer-aided word-search program, they were able to identify recurring themes which they later referenced as *Shared Values*.

Building off these initial studies and research, our own consulting work at Fired Up Culture with clients led to the formation of what we now call *the **Connected Values Framework**™*. The framework has proven to be universal, common to people all over the world regardless of nationality, race, religion, gender, industry, social status, or education. As we have measured engagement levels in the workplace, it represents the values people prize the most in the workplace.

CONNECTED VALUES
FRAMEWORK

Connected Values Framework™:

- To be able to tell the **truth** without fear, and to be told the truth
- To be able to **trust** their managers and co-workers, and to feel trusted
- To be confident that leaders and co-workers are **honest** *and ethical*
- To experience **respect** from their colleagues
- To give and receive **mentoring** **or coaching** without people becoming defensive
- To see managers and co-workers as **open** *to new ideas*
- To feel safe being **courageous** both personally and organizationally
- To be given credit and to **give credit** *when it is due*
- To know that **selfless behavior** is celebrated and rewarded

The Foundation of Values

Values are the "windows" through which our decisions are made. Influenced by a variety of factors, values subconsciously drive our thoughts, attitudes and actions, most of the time without us even recognizing it.

Conflict, major disagreement and/or allegations of disrespectful behavior can often be attributed to differences in values systems.

When we feel that are values are being questioned, challenged or attacked, we tend to respond by defending our own values. This causes us to lose sight of our common goals, and instead, focus on defending who we are as individuals, rather than attempting to resolve conflict with our relationships.

Truth: The Ability to Have the Hard Conversation

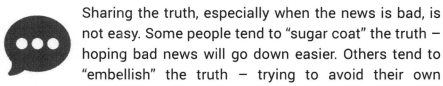 Sharing the truth, especially when the news is bad, is not easy. Some people tend to "sugar coat" the truth – hoping bad news will go down easier. Others tend to "embellish" the truth – trying to avoid their own blameworthiness for bad news by exaggerating the culpability of others. A more productive approach to truth-telling is to tell the uncompromising truth without embellishment or trying to make the truth less unpleasant.

The shared value of truth comes to life when issues are addressed within 24 hours of the event. When it comes to the truth, it's critical that we work through issues in real-time and by keeping short accounts. Ignoring issues, letting them build, hoping an issue will go away, or thinking you can avoid blame by keeping your mouth shut are not effective strategies.

The truth nearly always comes to light, and when it becomes clear to those who have been kept in the dark that you failed to tell the truth, they feel betrayed. It's far better to share bad news in a timely manner. As a general guide, within 24 hours.

Obviously, there are times when any delay, even a few minutes, is inappropriate; and there are times, when allowing a couple of days to pass might make sense. A good rule of thumb is to ask yourself: "How soon would I want to hear the truth myself?"

Coaching Corner

Skills for Having the Hard Conversation

- **Ask Permission**

  Before delivering the truth, ask the person you need to talk to, "Is this a good time to talk?" Using a phrase like this shows respect (another shared value) for the time and priorities of the other person. Adopting the phrase "Is this a good time to talk?" becomes code to everyone in the organization that you have something important to discuss, something that really can't wait. Using the phrase signals to the other person that you need their undivided attention and that finding an appropriate place to discuss the matter is important.

- **Set the Environment**

  Approach the other person in a non-threatening way. In other words, be sure that your approach doesn't put the other person on the defensive. Of course, being aware of factors that may put the other person on the defensive is important. This might include aggressive body language or tone of voice. Your physical size or gender may also be threatening. Even the location you choose for sharing your truth can be important. Delivering the hard news privately tends to also set the conversation up for success.

- **Keep It Simple & Focused**

  It's very important to make it clear that your intention is to discuss the issue, not to place blame. Be very straightforward about the issue. Make sure your language is simple, understandable and non-personal; and be sure to steer clear of becoming defensive yourself. Avoid sharing the truth in such a way that it's heard by the other person as a complaint or a demand. Instead, after you've brought the issue forward, make a request of the other person. Ask for their help in choosing an appropriate course of action.

Trust: The Bedrock of Sustainable Relationships

 Building and sustaining trust requires effective two-way communication among the members of the management team, between managers and workers, and among colleagues. Lavishing trust means that people throughout the organization at every level are trusted to take on new responsibilities and to complete projects without needing to be supervised. Trust is supported by three pillars: *competency, communication,* and *character.*

The first pillar – *competency* – is the expectation that you understand how to do the tasks necessary to get the job done. While you may lack experience, you at least need enough basic knowledge to perform the tasks without someone checking up on you. Don't let the person who's trusting you to do the job abandon you. Ask that person to make themself available to help whenever you ask for help.

The second pillar of trust – *communication* – is the expectation that you will communicate with the person who's trusted you both while you're working on the project, and at its completion. Memos, emails, voice messages, and reports are inadequate; two-way, face-to-face interaction is the most effective. Earning someone's trust requires that you to clearly understand their expectations. Restate their expectations in your own words so that they have an opportunity to clarify if necessary. Once you're confident that you clearly understand their expectations, ask to be given the freedom to find your own way to complete the work, even when you appear to be struggling.

The third pillar of trust – *character* – is the expectation that we possess the character that merits the trust of others, in other words, that we're ethical. Russell Gough, Professor of Ethics and Philosophy at Pepperdine University asserts that character is a *choice*: "Despite the fatalistic 'I can't help it' attitudes so prevalent in our day, the truth is that we do have control over and can overcome our weaknesses of character."[5] So, in order to become trustworthy, you must be willing to *choose* to be trustworthy, especially if people think you've not been untrustworthy in the past.

Earning the trust of others requires that you to prove your trustworthiness every day by being responsible and accountable. Before taking on a new task, reach agreement on a completion date or time and what the finished job will look like. Make it clear that you've *willingly* accepted responsibility for the task. Playing the passive-aggressive game of letting someone *assume* you've agreed to take on a task, and then claiming later that you never actually agreed to, is a choice that demonstrates a lack of character.

Honesty: Living Consistently with a Moral Compass

 People who are caught committing corporate wrongdoing like theft of petty cash, embezzlement, or fraud, often report when they are arrested, "I never intended to steal from the company." The story they often tell is that they were facing some personal financial crisis that required a temporary loan of company funds that they always intended to pay back.

Their co-workers say they're shocked that their friend would do such a thing. They would never admit that they were aware of the theft, or at least suspected that something wrong was going on. Let's be honest: it's tough to confront a co-worker you suspect has done something wrong or if you've actually seen them do something wrong. It's easier to shake your head and look the other way.

Imagine seeing someone walking out the door with a box of office supplies or conducting personal business on company time. Should you confront them? Or, because "it's no big deal," or "everybody's doing it," should you let it go?

The hard truth is that knowing about wrongdoing and failing to either confront the offender or report it makes you complicit, whether you choose to become involved in the unethical activity or not. Unethical or dishonest behavior includes more than theft or fraud; simply failing to put in an honest day's work is a form of dishonesty too. And yet, disgruntled workers all over the globe engage in a game of "catch me if you can" with their managers. They work hard only when being directly supervised and lazing around whenever they're not.

Honesty and ethics provide the bedrock of pride in an organization. When people adhere to high standards of corporate ethics that are non-negotiable, when they clearly support their organization's values, when people put in an honest day's work every day, when they take pride in their organization's products and services, and when people are willing to confront dishonest and unethical behavior is all of its forms, an "*Own It Culture*" becomes possible.

Respect: Being Accepted for Who I am

Respect is a key requirement for a healthy work environment. It promotes teamwork and increases productivity and efficiencies. It lets employees know they're valued for their abilities, qualities, and achievements, and that their role is important to their company's success. Being respected and valued promotes a positive work culture where employees are loyal, fulfilled, and motivated to perform at their best for their company. People who are not respectful to others are unprofessional and a threat to the health of their company.

We judge respect by the way our organization, superiors, and co-workers treat us. It's apparent in how the organization establishes new rules and policies and introduces them to employees, and how they compensate, recognize, and reward. Respect can also be determined by how often workers are asked their opinion, consulted about any changes that could affect their jobs prior to being implementing, and meaningful projects are assigned.

Respect is a stress reducer. A respected employee no longer has reason to fear being stepped on or stepped over. When another person experiences respect, they have freedom – freedom to perform without the worry of being the subject of gossip and ridicule. The respected person is also free to be themselves and to live and work within their own skin, without the stress of feeling they have to please everyone around them. They no longer have the stress of trying to be someone they're not.

One of the best ways to demonstrate respect in the workplace is to genuinely take the thoughts and opinions of people into consideration when making decisions that could impact them. Doing so lets people know that they matter. Feeling part of process provides people with an internal motivation.

Mentoring: Investing in Those Around Us

Mentoring relationships are a dynamic way to share knowledge and experience throughout the organization.

Max DePree, former CEO of Herman Miller (famous for the *Aeron Chair*) writes: "The best people working for organizations are like volunteers. Since they could probably find good jobs in any number of groups, they choose to work somewhere for reasons less tangible than salary or position. Volunteers do not need contracts, they need covenants. Covenantal relationships enable corporations and institutions to be hospitable to the unusual person and to unusual ideas. Covenantal relationships enable participation to be practiced and inclusive groups to be formed."[6]

Mentoring is a covenantal relationship. So, before offering to be a mentor, always ask the other person for their permission. This can be accomplished by simply asking: "May I mentor you?" or May I help you?" By simply offering to mentor as a friend, you send the message that you're doing so because you enjoy helping them grow and learn, rather than to gain a political ally or as a disguise for supervision.

Mentoring is available all around you: from more experienced and knowledgeable colleagues, and from new colleagues with a fresh perspective. If someone has offered to mentor you, accept their help without becoming defensive. Give your express permission to be mentored. Be open to mentoring from anyone, whatever their rank or role in the organization. Often times, younger or less experienced co-workers may have surprising experience or knowledge that we lack.

Traditionally, a mentor is a senior, more experienced person entering into an extended mentoring relationship with a junior, less experienced protégé. You've probably been in a relationship like this at some point in your life. Either you've been mentored by someone (perhaps a parent, teacher, experienced co-worker or boss) who has taken you under their wing and they've taught you a great deal, or you've been a mentor to someone. As helpful as these relationships can be, the mentor-protégé relationship is typically a power-based relationship, in which the protégé is dependent on or subordinate to the mentor.

A mentoring relationship in an *"Own It Culture"* is more of a long-term peer-to-peer relationship where both the mentor and person seeking mentoring choose each other. In order for a mentoring relationship to be sustained in this way, both parties must benefit.

The person seeking a mentor should benefit from becoming better at taking risks, experiencing a sense of progress, gaining confidence, developing a sense of purpose, and learning to become self-directed.

Likewise, the mentor should benefit from sharpening mentoring skills, gaining a skilled and confident partner, and above all, experiencing the joy of watching the person they are mentoring learn and grow.

Openness: A Willingness to Hear

New ideas are the key to continuous improvement and innovation. New ideas allow organizations to remove roadblocks, improve processes and delight customers. Yet, many organizations seem to purposely create roadblocks to new ideas. A complicated idea-submission and review-process makes it very difficult for new ideas to be brought forward and adopted. Layers of supervision in a hierarchical organizational structure make getting new ideas to move from the bottom to the top almost impossible. Structures that allow only senior executives to approve new ideas kill most innovative ideas in their infancy. As a result, in most organizations people on the front lines learn to keep their new ideas to themselves or to just stop using their innate intelligence.

Robert Sternberg, professor of psychology and Director of the PACE Center (Psychology of Abilities, Competencies and Expertise) at Tufts University contends that there are really three kinds of intelligence: *analytical* intelligence (the kind we measure with IQ tests), *creative* intelligence (the kind required for innovation) and *practical* intelligence (simple common sense).

"The most successfully intelligent people," says Professor Sternberg, "are not necessarily the ones with the greatest degree of intelligence in any of its three forms. But whether in school or the workplace, they're able to capitalize on their strengths, compensate for their weaknesses, and make the most of their abilities."[7]

Being open to new ideas requires a receptive mind – regardless of the origin of ideas. There are a number of factors that might close your mind to new ideas. You may rationalize, by offering what seem to you apparently reasonable explanations as to why other people's ideas won't work. You might allow your personal biases, like your dislike or disrespect for certain individuals or groups, to close your mind. You may use playing devil's advocate as a way to subtly communicate to others that you think they're less intelligent than you, and therefore less likely to have good ideas.

To show your receptivity, listen to new ideas with an open mind regardless of who is offering them. Restate the ideas in your own words so that those offering them can clarify. Set aside your personal biases and avoid putting people or their ideas down. Instead, ask reality testing questions to help make new ideas more successful.

Enthusiastically support new ideas that have been adopted, even when you're unsure of their opportunity for success, doing all that you can to help the new idea succeed.

Courage: The Willingness to Risk

Remaining competitive in tough economic times requires a culture that encourages risk-taking: an environment where people not only step forward with new and innovative ideas but are courageous enough to act on the strength of their convictions to do what's right. Remaining competitive requires organizations to give their complete and undivided attention to finding innovative ways to keep customers coming back and creative ways to bring in new ones.

Making it safe for individuals and teams to be courageous and take risks can only happen when you take steps to make it so. It's not enough to simply announce that it's safe to think "out of the box," i.e., to take personal risk for the organization's sake. You must encourage risk-taking by publicly recognizing and rewarding out-of-the-box thinking by visibly supporting courageous behaviors and celebrating them.

Beyond this, you need to take steps to uncover and remove any barriers to risk-taking, such as old-fashioned policies, procedures, processes, and systems that stand in the way of creating customer value. Furthermore, you need to encourage everyone in the organization to take the personal risk of challenging any and all barriers to customer value.

The more mature an organization is, the longer it's been in business. This means a greater possibility that the culture has become risk averse. Unlike entrepreneurial start-up companies that are typically experimenting and innovating just to survive, mature organizations have likely found a of formula that has brought them some measure of success. But as experience has taught us, past success is no guarantee of future success.

The trash heap of history is filled with mature organizations that failed to adapt fast enough to changing market conditions because their cultures stifled entrepreneurial risk-taking. Challenging long-standing policies and processes is often politically risky. It takes real courage to do this, because in most organizations it's not safe to do so.

Coaching Corner - Values

Values are defined as:

- Something that carries a significant amount of importance.

- Intrinsically valuable and desirable.

- Key to motivation, self-determination, resolution of conflict, and a purposeful life.

Our values can significantly influence how we process information and the decisions we make. Ideally, our values have been contemplated.

The term "Values" refers to something that is...

- chosen freely

- chosen from alternatives

- chosen after considering the consequences

- acted upon

- publicly affirmed

- pattern of life

We encourage you to spend a significant amount of time working through your organizational and personal values. The Connected Values Framework™ is a starting place. Making them real and applicable to you and your workplace are essential foundations for success. I explore values more specifically in our book series *Would You Work for You*.

More information on this book and support resources around values development can be found by visiting:

www.wouldyouworkforyou.firedupculture.com

Giving Credit: Celebrating the Success of Others

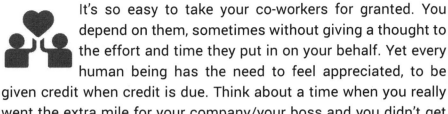It's so easy to take your co-workers for granted. You depend on them, sometimes without giving a thought to the effort and time they put in on your behalf. Yet every human being has the need to feel appreciated, to be given credit when credit is due. Think about a time when you really went the extra mile for your company/your boss and you didn't get so much as a "thank you".

Or worse, you developed a new idea or completed a really challenging project only to see someone else take credit for it. How did you feel? Would you ever put that much time and effort into a project for their benefit again? Now, think for a moment about a time when some individuals expressed heartfelt gratitude for your exceptional efforts on their behalf. How did you feel then? How did it influence your attitude toward them and the likelihood of putting forward that kind of effort again in the future?

We all want credit when credit is due. But is there a right way to give credit? Yes, there is. When you give credit to someone, take care that the praise you give is appropriate, genuine and fair. Appropriate praise is given in proportion to the contribution, small tokens of praise for small everyday contributions. In most cases, a simple "thank you" works just fine. For larger contributions, appropriate praise is public: either verbally or in writing.

Genuine praise comes from the heart; false praise is given for other reasons, such as for political gain or manipulation. Also, giving credit to others should be done fairly, regardless of status or role in the organization. It's very disheartening for an individual who has worked hard and made a significant contribution to stand by while their colleagues or their boss receives a bonus, a raise, or a promotion.

Selflessness: The Act of Being Concerned with The Needs of Others

 Selfless behavior, i.e., putting the interests of others before your own, may seem out of place in an organizational setting. But unless your colleagues and your customers feel you're considering their needs, eventually they will stop doing business with you. When asked, "What are the traits of the people you most admire?" people tend put together a list something like this:

- Openness
- Honesty
- Trustworthiness
- Courage
- Caring attitude
- Selflessness
- Sensitivity
- Good listening skills
- Truthfulness
- Encouragement
- Vision
- Knowledge

Did you notice that only the last trait on the list would be considered a technical skill? All of the others describe selfless behavior; behavior that puts the good of others ahead of self-interest.

Family therapist, Rosamund Stone-Zander and her husband, the world-renowned orchestral conductor, Benjamin Zander, in their book, *The Art of Possibility*, write about the importance of creating communities of people who put 'We' ahead of 'Us' and 'Them.'

"More often than not, history is a record of conflict between Us and Them. We see this pattern expressed across a broad spectrum: nation to nation, among political parties, between labor and management, and in the most intimate realms of our lives... The We appears when, for the moment, we set aside the story of fear, competition, and struggle, and tell its story. The We story... points to relationship rather than to individuals... [it is] the vital entity of our company, or community, or group of two."[8]

Choosing to be selfless does not oblige you to become a martyr or someone's door mat. It simply requires you to fully engage yourself in promoting community – in the We – by helping others succeed and celebrating their success even when there is no personal benefit to doing so.

Reducing the "Values Gap"

What is the "values gap"? A values gap is the interpersonal conflict that results when there is a gap between what people expect regarding the *Connected Values Framework*™ and what they actually observe from their managers and co-workers. In organizations where the values gap is high, productivity and profits suffer. In organizations where the gap is low, measures of operational success are consistently higher.

Our work around the *Connected Values Framework*™ continues to clearly show the importance of these values to people in all industries and all cultures worldwide. We believe there is a direct correlation between these values and overall organizational success. In our consulting work at *Fired Up! Culture*, we've tested the theory across our client base. Specifically, we completed a case study on a small pilot group of service firms across the United States.

This small study confirmed a direct link between values outlined in the Connected Values Framework™ and each organization's bottom line. Since then, hundreds of organizations and operational units have been studied by *Fired Up! Culture* and a strong correlation between the *Connected Values Framework*™ and operational results has been confirmed. When present, these values help to create an *Own It*™ or *Take Responsibility Culture*, and enable people perform at their best.

Connected values are the foundations which an *Own It Culture* are built on. Based on the results of more than 20 years of consulting and organizational change work, we clearly see the connection between the values gap and organizational success by comparing the values gap scores against measures of organization success, such as profits and productivity.

It's easy to understand why this connection exists. Think about it. When you're working in a culture where the level of interpersonal tension is high, a great deal of your energy is used on avoiding or dealing with conflicts that inevitably erupt. Dealing with constant interpersonal conflict distracts and discourages you from spending your energy on productive activities like completing important projects and tasks, solving problems, and giving your customers your undivided attention.

In addition to this, interpersonal conflict is stressful, and stress negatively impacts both your mental capacity and your physical endurance. In contrast, when the level of interpersonal tension is low, your interactions with co-workers are smoother and easier. You and your co-workers are more energetic and more focused on your customers, on improving your systems, and on solving problems.

If we put pressure on an organization, or the people working in the environment, we'll soon see where the cracks exist. A culture survey, and subsequently measuring any values gaps, will help highlight where potential cracks exist and allow leaders to proactively address the challenges.

Like the results of the original pilot group, each organization that completes the *Fired Up! Culture Index* is encouraged to compare the values gap scores of each department, team, or location with their operational results. Over the years the *Fired Up! Culture* team has been able to confirm a high correlation between the values gap and operational results.

Perhaps more interestingly, *Fired Up! Culture* has also noticed that a values gap is also a highly reliable predictor of the organization's success in the following year. A low values gap score does not *guarantee* future success. After all, there are many factors that impact on an organization's success, i.e., global pandemics, changing market conditions, changes in customer preferences, and of course, the overall economy.

In simple terms, organizations with a low values gap score have a much better chance for survival when business conditions are tough simply because their culture is healthier and therefore better able to adapt to challenges.

Increasing Team Member Engagement

When asked, most people in an organization would tell you that they're working hard and fully engaged in their work. From my vantage point, I know very few people who get up in the morning wanting to fail at their jobs. However, often what people *intend* to do and what they *actually* do are two different things. While they might intend to behave as good team members or independent idea generators, others might see them as people who are just going through the motions, or who are angry and frustrated.

Can you expect people, who appear not to be fully engaged in their work, to become fully engaged? Yes, but you must close the gap between their intended behavior and their actual behavior.

The *Fired Up! Culture Index* measures this gap by asking people first to describe how engaged they are, and then to describe how engaged their co-workers are. They're given four types of behavior to choose from:

1. A *champion* who is fully engaged with their team (Fired Up).  **CHAMPION**

2. A *maverick* who is less engaged with the team yet is fully engaged in their work (Igniting).  **A MAVERICK**

3. A **marginally engaged** nine-to-fiver who does what is asked each day (Smoldering).  **MARGINALLY ENGAGED**

4. Or a **mostly disengaged** dissenter who has become frustrated and angry (Burnt Out).  **MOSTLY DISENGAGED**

In the average organization, about 85% of team member see themselves as either a hero or a maverick (fully engaged); while on average, only 42% see their co-workers as fully engaged.

You may be surprised to hear that only 42% see their co-workers as fully engaged. This statistic reminds me of the old joke about the woman who has been working at a new job for about a month. When she's asked by her spouse a simple question: "How many people work at your company?" Not knowing the answer, the next day she asks a co-worker this question, as they had been with the company for a long time. The veteran employee thinks for a moment and then wryly replies, "Oh I don't know, I'd guess about half." It turns out that while most of us see ourselves as fully engaged, we are inclined to see others as less engaged than ourselves. The *Fired Up! Culture Index* confirms this perceived gap.

The *Fired Up! Culture Index* shows that healthy organizations have a much narrower perception gap. Why is this? Perhaps because people working in an *Own It Culture* are given the freedom of working in self-managing team. This means they're much more aware of how engaged their co-workers really are. It's also highly likely that workers in these healthier environments *really are* more engaged in their work.

Igniting Intrinsic Motivation

In the early 1930s, B. F. Skinner, a brilliant professor of psychology at Harvard, developed the theory of motivation he called, "Operant conditioning." Based on his experiments where he changed the behavior of rats and pigeons by conditioning them to expect a reward for a desired behavior or a punishment for an undesirable behavior, Skinner concluded that changing human behavior could be similarly accomplished.

In Skinner's own words: "Find the right stimulus and you'll get the desired response."[9] Skinner's theory of human motivation became the justification for industry, government and education to embrace incentives whole-heartedly.

But do incentives really motivate? You bet they do!

Incentives appeal to the natural human desire for recognition and money. The problem is that using incentives as the default tool for motivating people to work harder implies that a lack of employee motivation is the main cause of substandard individual performance and engagement.

Challenging the assumption that incentives are an effective tool, the conclusions of numerous independent studies over the last several decades have shown that incentives do more harm than good.

Incentives do motivate: they motivate people to earn more incentives, while often ignoring or overlooking the negative side effects.

Alfie Kohn, noted author and expert on the toxic side effects of incentives, summarizes the argument against using incentives this way: "While manipulating people with incentives seems to work in the short run, it is a strategy that ultimately fails and even does lasting harm."[10]

In his powerful book on the subject of how incentives affect human motivation, *Punished by Rewards,* Kohn presents the conclusions of several researchers who've extensively studied the subject. The researchers discovered convincing evidence that Skinner's theory of using incentives to drive human behavior is seriously flawed. While they agree that offering a reward (or punishment) influences human behavior in the short term, they found that motivating long-term behavior is much more complex than Skinner's theory would lead us to believe.

In fact, people being offered an incentive for an activity tend, over time, to lose interest in those activities, even if they previously had enjoyed doing them without the incentive. People became less intrinsically motivated, that is, less engaged in tasks because they felt manipulated by the incentive.

Even more startling is that the researchers found that a high percentage of subjects who were offered an incentive either did the minimum required to earn it, or worse, they cheated. In short, incentives tend, in the long run, to discourage workers from staying engaged and excited about their work.

In a brilliant book, *Drive – The Surprising Truth About What Motivates Us,* author Daniel Pink describes motivation as falling into three categories:

- Motivation 1.0 is the motivation to meet our basic needs for survival – food, water, air, shelter, and safety.
- Motivation 2.0 is the use of carrots and sticks to coax people to do unpleasant or repetitive tasks.
- Motivation 3.0 is intrinsic motivation driven by three things:

  o **Autonomy** – the ability to be self-directed.
  o **Mastery** – the desire to get better and better at something that matters.
  o **Purpose** – pursing a cause greater and more enduring than yourself.

Pink uses another pair of powerful metaphors to describe motivation: *"Type X Behavior* – behavior fueled more by extrinsic desires than intrinsic ones and concerned less with the inherent satisfaction of an activity and more with the external rewards to which an activity leads,"* and *"Type I Behavior* – behavior [that] concerns itself less with the external rewards an activity brings and more with the inherent satisfaction of the activity itself."[11]

Our work, more specifically the data coming from our culture survey processes, has confirmed that the most effective motivation for workers isn't the extrinsic incentives of good wages and job security; the most effective workplace motivator is intrinsic –*interesting work.*

Of course, the financial rewards need to be adequate to attract and retain the best talent available. But money is not enough to keep talented people motivated. People crave work that is challenging, rewarding and exciting. They need to feel their efforts are significant, and they want an opportunity to really make a difference.

Coaching Corner - Values

The *Connected Values Framework*", *and* specifically the identified values, were the key themes identified by researchers who were studying the literal comments of 17 million survey responses from people in 40 countries. A positive correlation between the values gap and operational results has been validated with the data from the *Fired Up! Culture Index*".

The values gap is a measure of the interpersonal conflict that results when there is a gap between what people expect regarding the connected values and what they actually observe from their leadership and co-workers. When the values gap is high, operational results suffer. When values gap is low, operational results improve.

Employee engagement improves when people have the freedom to manage themselves and to work together in self-managing teams. Motivation improves when people have work that is challenging, rewarding, and exciting.

The *Fired Up! Culture Index*™ is one of the most comprehensive measure of workplace wellness and engagement available. With more than 15 years of data and more organizations being added daily, the organizational change experts at *Fired Up! Culture* have created a series of workplace culture indexes which, by measuring the values gap, motivation, employee engagement, and leadership impact, can accurately predict how well the organization will perform in terms of operational and financial results.

For more information visit our website at www.firedupculture.com or call us at 855.9.FIRE.UP (1-855-934-7387).

CHAPTER 3

Own It:
Eliminating
Toxic Behaviors

"

*The way you see people
is how you treat them
and how you treat them
is what they become."*
– Goethe

One of the thorniest challenges facing organizations that are trying to establish an *Own It Culture*™ is confronting and overcoming behaviors that inhibit responsibility-taking. These behaviors are easy enough to spot in others, especially a boss or co-worker.

However, they're tougher to admit about ourselves. Despite our best efforts to interact with co-workers as respected peers, we may find ourselves caught up in Machiavellian behavior patterns of power and control. Put bluntly, we're talking about any behavior that is bullying.

According to Niccolò Machiavelli, author of *The Prince*, "A good prince may take any action, no matter how cruel or unjust, as long as his action maintains the stability of the principality he rules". It is vital, Machiavelli goes on, that a prince does anything necessary to keep his power, concluding, "It is best to be both feared and loved; however, if one cannot be both it is better to be feared than loved."[12]

Unfortunately, "Machiavellian" is a good description of how many people tend to behave when working within toxic environments. To illustrate, let me share a personal story:

My wife and I were on a walk in our hometown in the Pacific Northwest when we bumped into a former elementary school teacher who had the pleasure of teaching our four children over the years. We've lived in this thriving but small community for over 30 years, so running into people you know is common. On this particular walk, our teacher friend, Rebeca, was walking with her husband Mike (not their real names).

While Rebeca and my wife filled each other in on how all the kids were doing, I chatted casually with Mike. Mike had been a coaching client several years back. He said to me, "I want to thank you for our coaching time together. I know it wasn't long (about a year) but frankly, it was life-giving. I mark my professional path as 'before coaching with Chris' and 'after'". He went on, and before my Chris time, I thought I might be crazy."

As a coaching client, I definitely knew the ins and outs of Mike, his style, what he values and the work environment he found himself working in. Let me fill you in.

Mike was a mid-level manager at a large government facility near our home. He described how, by using the frameworks and practices we worked through in his coaching program, his department had been doing very well. He had formed a self-managing team giving the members complete freedom to own their jobs without his supervision, to develop their own new ideas, and to find solutions to problems without checking with him.

As a result, his people were thriving, and his team was delivering excellent results for their clients. At the same time, Mike's boss and some of the other mid-level managers who also reported to his boss were operating on the conventional top-down management model. This is not uncommon in government or other highly structured organizations.

This resulted in a long list of toxic behaviors: political infighting, a growing list of targets imposed from the top, resistance to those targets from those at the bottom, and internal competition for resources. In short, they were not doing as well as Mike's team. What Mike found interesting was that his boss and many of the people in other departments were engaging in a broad range of toxic workplace behaviors. They didn't realize that by adopting Mike's philosophy, his boss and his fellow mid-level managers could soon put an end to those toxic behaviors and vastly improve their operational results.

To be fair to Mike's bosses, even if you intellectually understand the idea of a creating an *Own It™ Culture* by forming Self-Managing Teams and encouraging people to share leadership as Emergent Leaders, it's still very difficult to break free of power-based relationships and patterns of behavior when you've spent years in working in a hierarchical environment.

If you're in a position of authority, you might even see yourself as morally superior, while correcting the toxic behavior of your subordinates who seem to lack the moral compass you possess. If you're not in a position of authority, you may see yourself as powerless to change the bullying behaviors of your bosses.

A more effective approach is to learn to recognize and eliminate your own responsibility-inhibiting behaviors.

In these next two sections, I discuss five bullying behaviors and five learned helplessness behaviors that inhibit responsibility-taking.[13] In my work and as a leadership coach, these 10 behaviors are literally at the root of most frustrations and challenges in the workplace that I've seen.

The Cupboard of Toxic Concoctions

As you can see, this next section is called the "cupboard of toxic concoctions".

Individually, the ten behaviors each can carry enough toxins to be extremely lethal for relations. Start combining these toxic behaviors in the workplace and they can literally be destructive on results, the ability to collaborate, delivering on the promises to your customers, and most importantly, the engagement levels of every team member.

We will walk through descriptions of each behavior, and briefly discuss how to recognize and begin to change, if not eliminate, these behaviors. It's important to note that these behaviors are *coping mechanisms*. They all work at a basic level, usually in the short term, otherwise, people wouldn't use in them.

But in the long term, they don't work well, and more importantly, they all damage relationships and inhibit responsibility-taking.

One significant note. Of the many toxic behaviors that exist in our workplaces today, the ones listed here are related specifically to culture, engagement and relationships in our workplace culture. It's intended to be a guide for all of us to own how we are showing up so we can address them proactively.

One of the greatest toxins, sexual harassment, I will not be addressing here. Sexual harassment stands by itself. It's extremely destructive and should be dealt with in a very specific way. If have experienced sexual harassment, subtle or direct, from a leader or colleague, please work with your Human Resource team, the authorities or an independent professional who can support you through getting these issues brought to light and resolved.

Toxic Behaviors

#1 – The Verbal Attack

 Despite their best intentions, when trying to find a resolution to a particularly tough issue, there are times when people resort to verbally attacking a co-worker. Though they intend to stay in control, at some point they become so frustrated with other people's seeming lack of understanding or empathy for their point of view or frustrated with their inability to get their point across, or just plain impatient with other people, that they resort to personal attacks.

People who verbally attack may adopt a harsh tone of voice or even shout. In addition, their body language might become hostile – aggressively pointing a finger, getting into another's personal space or using other forms of physical or psychological intimidation. Their words may become sarcastic or insulting. They may even resort to name-calling, attacking others where they are most vulnerable.

Verbally attacking others is a way to vent frustrations. The person being attacked may have no direct connection to the underlying source of the attacker's frustration. Merely because the person is available and vulnerable, they may have the misfortune of being the object of attack. Although verbal bullying may make the attacker feel better for a moment and give them a sense of control, this behavior undeniably damages workplace relationships, often permanently.

If you find you have a tendency to verbally attack others, you need to acknowledge the true source of your frustrations: the personal disappointments and slights you feel you've had to endure. You may have grown up in a household or worked for years in an organization where you were the target of verbal attacks. Or, because you're frustrated and disappointed in yourself, but lack the courage to confront your own failures, you may transfer those failures onto the people you work with closely and see in them your own shortcomings.

The obvious antidote is to confront your failures and frustrations and address them, rather than attacking others. When you catch yourself verbally attacking someone, ask yourself, "Where is this behavior coming from? What's really going on here? What's really bothering me?"

When we're verbally battling with someone, we tend to see our own motivations and actions as pure, when in fact, our motivations are often very complex and often times, conflicting. The overall goal of this approach is creating a "Learning Conversation," where the focus moves you away from trying to persuade the other person that your version of events is the right one. It also moves us toward understanding the others person's point of view and solve the problem together.

Coaching Corner - Values

If you feel that you're being verbally attacked, a good model for addressing this behavior is the three-step *Difficult Conversations Model*[14] developed by the Harvard Negotiation Project.

The first step in the model is the "What Happened Conversation," in which you and the other person each explore your perceptions of what happened, the factors that might have contributed to the situation, and the impact on each of you.

The second step is the "Feelings Conversation", in which the goal is to address each of your feelings about what happened without judgment or attribution.

The third step is the "Identity Conversation," in which the goal is to understand the self-image issues that are at stake.

#2 – Keeping Score

 Keeping score is a strategy people use to gain allies with co-workers and bosses. Think about that for a moment. The whole idea of needing to score points to gain allies implies that there is some kind of highly competitive game or war going on within organizations.

Too often, there often is a war going on; a fierce competition that pits peers against peers for prestige, promotions, and pay increases. It's no surprise that this competitive environment and the associated scorekeeping damages workplace relationships by promoting internal rivalries between individuals and groups.

When people find themselves keeping score, it might be because they're working in an environment where no one gets something for nothing. They're likely to hear people saying things like, "I'll do this for you if you'll do that for me," and "You owe me." This "quid-pro-quo" approach of keeping score merely trades accumulated points for special treatment, much like corrupt elected officials trade votes for political favors.

Many organizations have also institutionalized internal competition in a variety of ways. Perhaps the most damaging is a performance appraisal system where ranks employees against one another, and awards bonuses, pay increases and promotions are based on these peer appraisals.

Scorekeeping behavior in the workplace can be greatly reduced by identifying and eliminating all forms of internal competition, such as sales contests, incentives and performance ranking systems. Still, even when organizations have taken steps to eliminate internal competition, some individuals will continue to engage in personal scorekeeping. If you find yourself doing this, consider that seeing your co-workers as competitors turns them into adversaries, perhaps even enemies. Admit that needing to outdo others may be an attempt to cover up your insecurity and bolster your ego.

To stop this toxic behavior completely, you need to get out of your denial about scorekeeping and agree to partner with co-workers, rather than compete with them. Take steps to build your self-esteem by improving your knowledge and skills. Volunteer to collaborate with co-workers to achieve a common goal rather than competing with them. Give credit to others whenever they make a contribution to the success of the group. Support others who take the personal risk of sharing ideas that may be unpopular and be willing to step up with ideas of your own. Ask for coaching from a co-worker whenever you need it and be willing to coach others whenever they ask for it.

Toxic scorekeeping should not be confused with appropriate forms of measuring progress that don't involve internal competition. People working in healthy organizations measure their progress continually. In fact, as I will discuss later, developing an appropriate group of measures is vital to your organization's success.

#3 – Finding Fault

 When problems occur, as they often do in every organization, you may notice that some people in your organization have a tendency to look for people to blame. Rather than looking at how the design of the systems might have contributed to problems, these people habitually look for a scapegoat. Looking for a person to blame (especially when it's most often the system that's at fault) is a waste of time and energy.

According to W. Edwards Deming, an American Engineer and management consultant considered the father of the workplace process improvement and quality movement, more than 95% of problems that occur in any system or process are a direct result of the design of the system. So, to reduce or eliminate problems, Deming advised leaders to look for the flaws in the system, not look for fault in the people working within the system.

People who have adopted the habit of finding fault in others. They might use words like "always" and "never," as in: "You _always_ do this" or "You _never_ do that". Of course, the truth is that these words are exaggerations and argumentative.

Faultfinders (i.e., people who always look for faults in others) may try to sugarcoat their habit by calling it "constructive criticism," offered to help others improve. Don't be fooled by this tactic. Constructive criticism is not often seen as constructive. It's most often perceived as personal and destructive: it strikes at the heart and wounds people.

A natural defense to criticism is to counterattack, turning the criticism back on the criticizer. This strategy, too, is unproductive, because it merely escalates faultfinding, and does nothing to move the conversation in a productive direction.

Finding fault in others when you feel you're not getting the results you want at work is very human. It's hard to break the natural tendency to do the easy thing: to seek out a scapegoat when you're not getting what you want at work. It's more difficult, but much more productive, to focus your attention on taking ownership for improving your own actions and behaviors, and the system you work in.

A more effective alternative is to reframe your thinking and focus your attention on the steps you need to take to solve problems without assigning blame to others.

#4 - Needing to be Right

For those people who have worked, or are working, in organizations that impose rigid policies and performance standards on employees, "needing to be right" isn't an option. It's an imperative. It springs from a need to be in control. Everything must be done the company way. The only ideas that are valid are management's ideas. The only way to do anything is the boss's way – no matter how well another way might work.

The person who needs to be right operates by a different set of rules. They believe if you're in a position of authority, it's your job to decide what to do, when and how to do it, and why it should be done. And above all, they believe (falsely) that if you're in charge, never admit when you're wrong.

People who've taken on the habit of needing to be right might camouflage it by interrupting others, so that they're unable to finish explaining their ideas or sulking and playing the martyr when their ideas are challenged. They might try to use guilt to induce others to give in to their "rightness," and in so doing, manipulate others into doing their bidding. They may masquerade as someone who has an elevated level of self-confidence and competence in order to get others to go along with them. All of these behaviors are a smoke screen to allow them to delude themselves into believing they are morally superior to everyone else.

You might ask: isn't being in control (directing activity, and expecting things to be done the "right" way) what people in authority are supposed to do?

In a conventional management system, the answer is: yes. There is a difference in an *Own It Culture* where the objective is for everyone to own their jobs, own the systems and be accountable for delivering results. Always needing to be right is a toxic behavior.

To break this nasty habit, organizations must discard the whole notion of needing rigid policies and performance standards to control the behavior of people working in the system. Instead, they need to cultivate an environment where people are continually experimenting with better ways of doing things. Rather than trying to find that "one right way," a better strategy is to look for ways to continuously improve workflow and remove waste, so that the system can deliver more of what customers really want.

If you've acquired the habit of always needing to be right, you must first acknowledge your feelings of self-righteousness and moral superiority. Then, take a healthy dose of humility, and be prepared to admit you're not always right. If you're in a position of authority, create a work culture where experimenting is the norm. Of course, experimentation requires an open mindset where being wrong is a pathway to learning and finding workable solutions. Moreover, experimentation often leads to important discoveries that couldn't have occurred any other way. Above all, adopt the attitude that while you should always try to _do_ right, you do not always need to _be_ right.

#5 - Refusing to Forgive

 Refusing to forgive is a strategy people use to try to protect themselves from being hurt again. In refusing to forgive, some people construct an emotional wall around themselves which they wear like protective armor. Unfortunately, the resentment and bitterness they feel often become so prominent in their outward emotions that these emotions often spill over and poison the person's workplace relationships. In effect, refusing to forgive does more damage to the person and those closest to them, than it does to the person they refuse to forgive.

Here's how this toxic behavior looks: someone becomes so angry over what they view as the past transgressions of the offender that they explode over the smallest lapse. They might try to control the person who hurt them through shame by constantly reminding that person of their every imperfection, mistake or failure. They may refuse to forgive if the person who hurt them is not sorry enough, has not apologized enough, or has not done enough to make up for past offenses. They may interpret all of the alleged offender's statements and actions in a negative light. And, they may become very self-righteous, seeing themselves as completely blameless.

Refusing to forgive keeps you locked up emotionally. You become a prisoner to our own pain and give the person who hurt you power to continue to hurt. Although it's certainly not easy and it takes time and persistence, learning to forgive ultimately gives you the strength to break the bonds of your anger and pain. In the end, learning to forgive isn't just something you need to do for the benefit of those who have hurt you and the people closest to you; it's something you need to do for yourself.

The Cunning Craft of the Helpless

People who find themselves in a shaky situation, where they feel helpless to defend themselves, often fall into to a state of *learned helplessness*. We consider learned helplessness to be a toxic behavior of a different kind.

Philip Zimbardo writes in *The Lucifer Effect,* "Experiencing a loss of personal identity and subjected to arbitrary continual control of their behavior, as well as being deprived of privacy and sleep, generated in them [the young men playing the role of prisoner in the *Stanford Prison Experiment*] a *syndrome of passivity, dependency, and depression* that resembled what has been termed 'learned helplessness.'"[15]

Learned helplessness is a coping mechanism often observed in work environments where individuals have concluded that they're powerless to fight "the system" or those in authority over them. Unfortunately, learned helplessness is a coping mechanism with a high cost. Not only do people who choose learned helplessness often suffer a loss of personal identity, they also lose any sense of responsibility for their choices and actions.

Learned Helplessness Behaviors

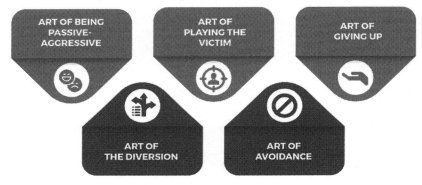

#6 - The Art of Being Passive-Aggressive

Passive-aggressive behavior, while passive on the surface, is aggressive behavior, nonetheless. When you see a master of passive-aggressive behavior, you see a person highly skilled at trickery and sabotage. They're always careful to cover their tracks so that they can maintain a high degree of deniability.

Put simply, passive-aggressive behavior is *devious.* In the workplace, you might see people using passive-aggressive behavior to indirectly obstruct those projects and people who oppose them or don't want them to succeed, even finding a way to quicken failure if they can. Catching someone in passive-aggressive behavior can be like trying to prove the existence of UFOs. Although you might have bits of evidence, you can never conclusively prove it. Even though you might have seen them doing something underhanded, proving that they intended the devious behavior is often nearly impossible.

If you confront someone about passive-aggressive behavior, they may have some kind of justification at the ready. When working with others on a problem, passive-aggressive individuals may let others make suggestions, but then find an indirect way of tearing the suggestion apart. When others suggest a change or an idea that passive-aggressive people don't like, they may pretend to be confused. Even if they may give the impression of a willingness to go along with an idea, they then find an indirect way to later sabotage the idea.

If forced to participate in tasks they don't like, passive-aggressive individuals might pretend to be inept, so they can manipulate others to step in and do it for them.

In organizations where passive-aggressive behavior occurs frequently, it's very likely that it's not safe to directly challenge authority. Passive-aggressive behavior most often occurs in authoritarian cultures where the need to be right is combined with a strong tendency to lay the blame for organizational failures on individuals.

In these cultures, employee feedback is often slanted toward the negative (such as focusing performance appraisals on improving weaknesses) and disciplinary tactics are in play (such as suspending workers without pay and withholding pay increases and promotions.) The obvious resolution to this situation is to move toward a more collegial culture of partnering where levels of mutual trust and respect are high, and where the truth is appreciated, even when the news is bad.

If you catch yourself engaged in passive-aggressive behavior, you need to stop yourself and choose instead to be up-front. Be honest about your thoughts and feelings so that you might convince your co-workers of your point of view. You should also be prepared to support your co-workers with an honest effort to make a project succeed, even when you still have reservations about their idea.

In short, if you have the habit of using passive-aggressive behavior, you need to stop playing games and start being more honest and straightforward.

#7 - The Art of the Diversion

 Diversions are a strategy people use to try to avoid talking about difficult issues. Using diversions, people hide their real concerns by talking about safe topics or arguing about one thing, when in reality they're really upset about something else.

For example, someone might criticize a co-worker for being too assertive in a meeting, when in reality they're really feeling insecure about their own assertiveness. They might get angry or withdraw if the discussion gets too close to real issues they don't want to discuss. They might talk passionately about resolving "other people's concerns." And then when pressed, they deny that these concerns are their own. When asked directly, "What's bothering you?" they become defensive, or shut down completely.

Because diversions hide your real agenda, it leaves co-workers confused. Co-workers take the diversions at face value and spend a great deal of energy trying to solve the problems being voiced. Yet, because the real issues are never brought forward, they can never be resolved. Diversions are bad for everybody. Co-workers grow more and more frustrated at their inability to adequately resolve the diversions; and the diverter grows increasingly frustrated that their co-workers never figure out what the real issue is, and therefore never resolve it.

It's tough to talk about your emotional issues, if you have them, when your real fear is that your concerns will be ignored or rejected, or that you will be ostracized. When your co-workers confront you about what's bothering you, rather than resorting to diversions, it's okay to say something like, "I'm not ready to talk about it yet; when I get my thoughts and feelings sorted out, I'll come talk to you. But right now, I'm asking you to give me some time."

Even when you know what's bothering you, it's hard not to get nervous and defensive and to fall back into diversions. It's okay to take the time to sort out your thoughts and feelings so that you can express yourself properly at a later time. Eventually, though, you need to find a safe setting where you can be up-front about your thoughts and feelings and be honest about what's bothering you.

#8 - The Art of Playing the Victim

 People are most likely to play the victim when they feel they're being treated unfairly. Playing the victim is fueled by a heightened sense of insecurity and vulnerability. When someone chooses the play the victim, they shift responsibility for their problems away from themselves onto someone else. They may look for reassurance from their friends and allies that their difficulties are the result of forces beyond their control. The more effective people are at playing the victim, the more subtly they are able to manipulate their co-workers into accepting their victimhood, and persuading colleagues to take responsibility for resolving their issues and problems, or perhaps even to save them.

When you play the victim, your co-workers become very tired of supporting you. You might think that by being meek and long-suffering, doing your best to get along, you're keeping the peace. Clearly this is not the case because your unquenchable need for reassurance means that your co-workers grow tired of your neediness.

And for those co-workers who are patient enough to continue to reassure you, they're in the position of having to give far more to the relationship than they receive. Your boss, too, grows tried of you playing the victim. Because of your unwillingness to step out of your victimhood, your boss is forced to make the choice between working around you and confronting you. Either choice requires extra time and effort.

Breaking free of playing the victim begins when you take responsibility for resolving your own issues and problems. It requires courage to face your personal insecurities and to take ownership for them. Playing the victim is a tough habit to break, especially when doing so has, at least to some degree, worked in the past.

The most effective way to break the habit is to acknowledge that you've been playing the victim and give your co-workers permission to "name it" when they catch you doing it. Often, simply being reminded by friends and co-workers who care about you that you're beginning to play the victim again, helps you to stop this behavior.

#9 - The Art of Avoidance

 "If I just ignore it, it will go away." While we laugh when we hear a character on a sit-com repeat these lines, hearing this at work it's not funny at all, because avoiding problems and sensitive issues at work doesn't make them go away.

In fact, in most cases, avoiding them often makes the situation worse. In spite of this, avoidance is a toxic behavior people use with alarming frequency. The syndrome of "avoiding" comes in many forms: people might avoid taking any action that might challenge that status quo of shaky, yet stable, workplace relationships.

They may avoid talking about the changes they want from a relationship with a co-worker because they've decided it's not worth the effort. If challenged by their co-workers about their avoiding behavior, they might say something like, "I don't need to change – you do!"

Avoiding issues and problems is clearly not an effective workplace behavior. If you have difficulties, you may find that rather than making your problems go away, avoiding allows your problems to persist or even escalate. To stop this behavior, you need to get out of denial and acknowledge that avoidance damages your workplace relationships. You need to find the courage to confront and talk about your issues and problems. You also need to commit to making the changes in your behavior that will improve your workplace relationships and your ability to be a productive member of the group. In short, you need to stop avoiding and start confronting your issues directly.

#10 - The Art of Giving Up

Giving up is the strategy of last resort. When people give up, they see themselves as helpless, caught in circumstances that are unchangeable and beyond their control. They see no way out and shut down completely. They give up on relationships with a co-worker and just "go through the motions" with them. They no longer protest when that person abuses them. They find it pointless to change because they believe that any change they make will only make things worse.

They find covert ways to avoid contact. In effect, they see no alternatives. What's surprising, however, is that people sometimes continue giving up, even if the situation has actually improved.

Learning to believe in the possibility of rebuilding a healthy relationship with a co-worker after having given up is very difficult, but it's not impossible. It starts when you resolve to hope again. It requires a willingness and desire to rebuild broken workplace relationships by changing your attitude about yourself and about your situation. It demands you to see yourself not as a helpless victim. You need to regard yourself as a self-directed autonomous individual, capable once again of shaping your relationships and your future.

Coaching Corner - Values

Learned Helplessness is a pattern of passivity, dependency, and depression brought on by a loss of personal identity in people subjected to arbitrary and continual control of their behavior. The syndromes of behaviors include being passive-aggressive, creating diversions, playing the victim, patterns of "avoiding," and giving up.

Part of creating a healthy workplace environment involves a willingness to confront and change your own learned helplessness. To assess the bullying and learned helplessness behaviors you currently see, complete the *Own It! Responsibility Inhibiting Behaviors (RIB) Self-Assessment* found by visiting our online resource page:

www.own-it-the-book.com/resources

As part of our *Leadership360* process, we have also built in the responsibility-inhibiting behaviors assessment so that clients can get feedback from colleagues about how they're showing up in the workplace.

More information on the *Fired Up Leadership360* process can be found by visiting the resource page listed above.

SECTION 2:

BUILDING AN OWN IT CULTURE

*"We should all have opportunities to feel a part of
something not just have a part in something."*
– Simon Sinek

In this Section:

- Emergent Leadership
- Making the Connections
- Assembling the Right Resources
- Coaching for Success - The TLC Method
- Creating Stewards of the Work
- More and Less Coaching Model

Ricardo Semler, the self-described "maverick" and CEO of Semco uses an exercise in leadership workshops he regularly conducts. He invites a group of volunteers to the stage to act out a survivor simulation where they're in an airplane that has crashed in the Himalayas. He appoints one of them as captain and then asks them to work out over the next 20 minutes what to do next.

Each time that he conducts this exercise, a leader (never the captain he's appointed) emerges who begins organizing the survivors into groups: "One assigned to looking for water, the other to fixing the radio or signaling passing airplanes, the third to tending the injured, and so on."

Semler describes what happens next: he interrupts the group and asks them to act out another scenario, and as he describes it, "This time an activist environmental group that had heard that a large chemical plant was going to dump toxic waste into the river that afternoon. Almost immediately, someone would take over as leader, and it was never the same person who had led the plane crash survivors... These exercises reinforced my belief that leadership indeed depends on the situation. As circumstances change, leadership must change. A certain set of skills, instincts, and personality traits may be perfect today, and become useless tomorrow."Semler observes: "At some point in the process, self-management takes over. Self-interest and the survival instinct kick in. The group coheres as its components start to function according to their unique skills tempered by experience. From then on leadership, beyond acting as a catalyst, directing traffic, and playing honest broker when conflicts arise, is superfluous. Moreover, in my view, obtrusive and intrusive leadership becomes counterproductive by interfering with the free interplay of individual talent and interest."16

These self-selecting leaders, leaders who have the courage to step forward with the "skills, instincts and personality traits" at precisely the right time are what I call: *Emergent Leaders.*

These Emergent Leaders don't necessarily need to be the person who's called "Manager" or "Supervisor". It's not about titles. Emergent Leaders can be anyone who has the knowledge and skills to fill a need that an individual or a group lack.

In short, Emergent Leaders step forward to share their skills and experience whenever leadership is needed.

Emergent Leaders do five key things which enable them to take leadership at the appropriate time. 1) Coach, 2) Counsel, 3) Connect People to Resources, 4) Encourage Stewardship, and 5) Help Others to See the Big Picture.

Emergent Leaders Coach

In an *Own It Culture*, when a person needs to learn something new, to gather information, or develop expertise and master new skills and proficiencies, an Emergent Leader steps up to offer coaching.

Emergent Leaders *Offer Counsel*

Once people turn their attention toward solving job-related problems and making day-to-day workplace decisions, Emergent Leaders make themselves available to offer counsel so that people can find their own solutions to everyday issues and problems.

Emergent Leaders *Connect People to Resources*

Having learned how to make decisions and solve problems independently, people in an *Own It Culture* begin to seek the resources they need to complete projects independently. Emergent Leaders connect their co-workers to the resources they need to meet these challenges.

Emergent Leaders *Encourage Stewardship*

Having mastered the art of securing resources, people are ready to assume ownership for their jobs and for the systems they work in. Emergent Leaders encourage their co-workers to become stewards of the organization.

Emergent Leaders *Help Others to See the Big Picture*

Every member of in an *Own It Culture* needs to understand how their job supports the larger purpose of the organization. To help make this important link, Emergent Leaders help their colleagues see the big picture by understanding how their individual and combined efforts contribute to the organization's success.

In this section we will explore how the Emergent Leader utilizes critical skills to build an *Own It Culture*, create deep engagement around the opportunity to take responsibility for the work, and how Emergent Leader's coach team members to a place of job ownership and successful results.

CHAPTER 4

Own It: Making the Connections

"

The way to get started
is to quit talking and
begin doing."
– Walt Disney

I n his book, *Let My People Go Surfing*, Yvon Chouinard, Founder and Owner of *Patagonia Inc*, describes how he made the transition from a lone entrepreneur tinkering in his workshop with rock-climbing equipment, to becoming the leader of an international manufacturer of environmentally friendly outdoor gear.

Chouinard characterizes his story as "the education of a reluctant businessman." In the introduction of his book, he describes the philosophy that has shaped his vision. Having grown up in the sixties, he had come to disdain big corporations and their "lackey governments," [i.e., conventional systems and structures.] "My values are a result of living a life close to nature."

Chouinard sees himself as a "contrarian," taking the lessons learned from living an "alternative lifestyle" and applying them to running a business.

"My company, Patagonia, Inc., is an experiment. We believe the accepted model of capitalism that necessitates endless growth and deserves the blame for the destruction of nature, must be displaced. Patagonia and its thousand employees have the means and the will to prove to the rest of the business world that doing the right thing makes for good and profitable business."

Chouinard's vision is that a company "can break the rules of traditional business and make it not just work but work even better..."[17]

A Compelling Case for Change

For Yvon Chouinard, change was called for when he realized one day that he wasn't merely an avid fan of the outdoors, making equipment that others wanted to use.

"I had always avoided thinking of myself as a businessman. I was a climber, a surfer, a kayaker, a skier, and a blacksmith." He continued the conversation to say that "One day it dawned on me that I *was* a businessman... It was also clear that in order to survive at this game, we had to get serious."

After experiencing tremendous expansion for several years Patagonia was experiencing growing pains.

"Looking back now, I see that we made all the classic mistakes of a growing company. We failed to provide the proper training for the new company leaders, and the strain of managing a company with eight autonomous product divisions and three channels of distribution exceeded management's skill. We never developed the mechanisms to encourage them to work together in ways that kept the overall business objectives in sight."

So, Patagonia's Leadership Coalition began making the changes and communicated those changes to the whole organization.

One of the most important new trends in the 21st century is that the most successful organizations in the world are moving away from conventional management thinking and moving toward an *Own It Culture*. CEOs are becoming keenly aware that the biggest threat to their organization is failing to make the change to an *Own It Culture* fast enough.

Therefore, they spend a good deal of energy creating a sense of urgency in an effort to shake people out of their complacency. Leaders throughout these organizations challenge the status quo by articulating a compelling case for change, identifying the problems associated with continuing on the organization's present path and spelling out the advantages of establishing an *Own It Culture*.

It turns out that the leaders of organizations that have adopted an *Own It Culture* as an operation principle are not superheroes who do it all themselves. Rather, they enlist the support of a *Leadership*

Coalition within the organization. Without the visible support of this Leadership Coalition, which includes senior leaders, middle leaders and front-line leaders who have become Emergent Leaders, the change to an *Own It Culture* is likely to fail.

The Leadership Coalition helps to make the case for change in a number of ways: they model non-authoritarian leadership, they encourage people to experiment, they make sure people are able to get the training they need, and they encourage greater levels of ownership.

In short, this Leadership Coalition makes the case for moving to an *Own It Culture* by "walking the talk" (I.e., actually doing what you say you will do).

Communicate the "Own It" Message

Patagonia has moved aggressively to create an *Own It Culture*; entrepreneurs within the company create products that solve the unique problems of outdoor enthusiasts like staying dry.

"At a time when the entire mountaineering community relied on the traditional, moisture-absorbing layers of cotton, wool, and down, we looked elsewhere for inspiration — and protection." So, creative thinkers at Patagonia developed the first polyester climbing sweater, and later climber's polypropylene underwear, which kept the climber both drier and warmer with fewer layers of clothing.

With tough competitors who copied their designs, Patagonia has been able to maintain their competitive edge by getting Emergent Leaders to take responsibility for continuously improving their products, always looking for ways to deliver more of what their customers want.

Making the change to an *Own It Culture* requires effective communication. In order to win hearts and minds, people in the organization need to be introduced to the idea of taking responsibility and understand the path to get there. Sending a memo, giving a speech or publishing an article in the company newsletter is insufficient. People need time to interact and discuss this new way of doing things in both formal and informal meetings.

Although meetings may be time consuming, costly and logistically difficult. Bringing people together to process and discuss the new philosophy is very important. Time away from their regular jobs allows people on the front lines time to understand and accept the idea of owning their jobs so they can successfully take ownership for their jobs and for becoming Emergent Leaders.

Repetition of the message is important. Advertising firms understand this very well. They never place a single advert; they develop an ad campaign that targets an audience and repeats the message often and in many different forms of media. So too, leaders understand that effective communication follows the old adage, "When you think they've got it, tell them again."

They know that the new philosophy needs to be heard many times before it sinks in; and people need to hear it from all members of the Leadership Coalition, not just the senior executives. Keeping in mind that actions speak louder than words, the behavior and actions of the entire Leadership Coalition must be consistent with the new responsibility-taking philosophy.

When inconsistencies surface, and they will, they need to be addressed. It takes time for the organization's systems and structures to change. It becomes evident very quickly that conventional top-down operating systems are not designed to support an *Own It Culture*. The Leadership Coalition needs to acknowledge these inconsistencies and encourage the members to challenge them.

Overcome Complacency

Overcoming complacency is one the biggest obstacles to this change. There are many reasons for complacency. One reason is that people have seen change initiatives come and go, and most have failed to deliver results as promised. People have a good reason to be skeptical. Most change initiatives don't work – not because the ideas are necessarily invalid or poorly conceived, but because they get the change process backwards.

They begin by trying to change the behavior of people rather than changing the system itself. It turns out that Deming was right. 95% of problems are caused by the system, not by people. So, establishing an *Own It Culture* focuses on changing the systems and structures rather than on changing people.

Chouinard understands the dangers of complacency very well. "After all those years of 30% to 50% compound annual growth and trying to have it all, Patagonia hit the wall."

With the country in recession, dealers were cancelling orders, inventory grew, their credit line was significantly reduced, and Patagonia was forced, for the first time in its history, to lay people off, which the management team hated doing. "We had never laid people off simply to reduce overhead. In fact, we had never laid anyone off for any reason. Not only was the company like an extended family, for many it was a family, because we had always hired friends, friends of friends, and their relatives."

Finally, the company had to let 120 people go, which was 20% of the workforce. Like so many organizations before, "We were forced to rethink our priorities and institute new practices." In short, they were shaken out of complacency and began to make real progress toward taking responsibility.

The Leadership Coalition needs to be prepared to break through significant obstacles and roadblocks to an *Own It Culture*. Not the least of these obstacles is the existing organizational structure. A conventional top-down organizational structure delegates responsibility downward and ensures accountability through a system of direct supervision, performance reports and periodic audits. The difference in an *Own It Culture* is that everyone is expected to be both responsible and accountable to each other, to the organization, and most of all, to their customers.

Breaking out of command-and-control thinking and the requisite need for layers of supervision and serial audits is a tremendous leap for leaders and workers. Especially those who have lived in this kind of environment for most of their adult lives.

Create a Sense of Real Progress

Chouinard understands the importance of a sense of progress very well. As the company recovered from their brief, but nearly fatal business slow-down, he decided to teach his team member part of what he had learned as a student of Zen philosophy.

"In Zen archery, for example, you forget about the goal – hitting the bull's eye – and instead focus on all the individual movements involved in shooting an arrow. You practice your stance, reaching back and smoothly pulling an arrow out of the quiver, notching it on the string, controlling your breathing, and letting the arrow release itself. If you've perfected all the elements, you can't help hitting the center of the target. The same philosophy is true for climbing mountains. If you focus on the process of climbing, you'll end up on the summit. As it turns out, the perfect place I've found to apply this Zen philosophy is the business world."

In order to establish and keep up momentum and enthusiasm for the move toward an *Own It Culture*, people need to feel a sense of real progress and success. A good way to create a sense of real progress is to institutionalize the sharing of good news stories and discussions of lessons learned from failures through regularly scheduled *Application Meetings.*

Application Meetings are an opportunity for all members of the organization to gather together in small groups to talk about how the organization is progressing toward an *Own It Culture*. During the initial stages of the change, these Application Meetings should be held monthly, so everyone in the organization has a chance to hear about what's happening in other parts of the organization.

Application Meetings should not be off the cuff or ad hoc. They need to be carefully planned in advance and presented by members of the Leadership Coalition. During each monthly meeting, a senior leader gives a brief view from the top. Then, a mid-level leader teaches something that everyone in the organization needs to learn. Finally, a frontline Emergent Leader shares an *application issue* (a good news story or a failed experiment) and facilitates a discussion about lessons learned.

In just 90 minutes, everyone in the organization hears what's going on from the senior leadership's perspective, learns something new, and has an opportunity to discuss how well the organization is applying the essential elements of an *Own It Culture*.

Make the *Own It Culture* Stick

Patagonia has always understood the importance of finding ways to make the *Own It Culture* stick. During the 2008 recession, the days of uncontrolled growth for Patagonia were over. They found they needed new "models of stewardship and sustainability" against which to gauge their future progress.

So, they eliminated several layers of management and streamlined their systems. They adopted a controlled growth rate of about 5% a year and got serious about choosing raw materials for their clothing line that had the least damaging environmental impact. They were recognized for their turnaround, listed in *Working Mother* magazine as one of the "100 Best Companies to Work For," and many times historically have been ranked in the "Top 25 Medium Sized Businesses" by the *Great Place to Work® Institute* and the *Society for Human Resource Management*.

Making a new *Own It Culture* stick requires making real changes from a culture of autocracy and bureaucracy to a culture of mutual trust and accountability. This requires time and persistence. People need time to internalize an *Own It Culture*, both in terms of the leadership model and organizational structure. Making this transition often requires *years,* not weeks or months. Even when people understand and accept the new concepts, changing the basis of relationships is a slow and sometimes painful process.

Changing workplace relationships, particularly previously unhealthy relationships, requires changes in thinking, attitudes and behaviors on everyone's part. It's a process that can be very threatening to people's idea of who they are and what they stand for.

In short, making the transition takes courage.

Coaching Corner

Seeing the 'big picture' means keeping people's eyes on the horizon, letting people know what's ahead, and provide a compelling reason to go there. Doing so requires a *Leadership Coalition* that creates a compelling case for change, communicate effectively, overcome obstacles and roadblocks, create a sense of real progress, and help make the *Own It Culture* stick.

To assess how often you engage in the five actions of an Emergent Leader, we encourage you to complete *The Emergent Leader Self-Assessment* found on our resource page at *www.own-it-the-book.com/resources*

The Emergent Leader Self-Assessment is designed to help you first assess, and then periodically measure, your progress on increasing the frequency of Emergent Leader actions.

The first time you take the self-assessment, you will establish a benchmark you can gauge your progress against. Repeat the self-assessment as often as you like. The self-assessment is for your personal use; you need not share your results with anyone.

However, you might want to ask one or more trusted colleagues to evaluate your progress by reviewing your self-assessment with them and having them providing feedback on how you're showing up in the specific areas being measured by the Emergent Leader Assessment.

CHAPTER 5

Own It: Assembling the Right Resources

"

*Most obstacles melt
away when we make
up our minds to walk
boldly through them."
– Unknown*

t's been nearly 100 years since Frederick Taylor published *The Principles of Scientific Management.*[18] Taylor laid out a system which simplified jobs so that workers could easily be trained to perform tasks on an assembly line without having to think. It was the early days of the industrial revolution and businesses were just beginning to make the transition from an economy that had depended on skilled craftsmen who built products one at a time, to a bold new economic model where products were mass-produced.

Henry Ford, who applied Taylor's principles, dramatically improved productivity at the Ford plant by three to four times; and in so doing, reduced the cost of his Ford automobiles to an affordable level. Because of this incredible leap in productivity, Ford was able to dramatically raise the daily wage of his workers to a level where they could, for the first time, actually afford to purchase the automobiles they produced.

Before that time, handcrafted automobiles were accessible only to the very wealthy. There turned out to be a dark side of Taylorism for Ford's workers though. Because it had become so easy to train replacements using Taylor's scientific management system, workers lived under the constant threat of being fired should they fail to meet their daily quotas. While worker's pay had substantially increased, their jobs had become sheer drudgery, their bosses had become bullies, and they had no control over their daily tasks.

Using the principles of "Scientific Management", roles were established which separated the "thinking" reserved for senior executives and managers, from the "doing" assigned to labor.

What's the Problem? Hint, It's Not Your People

Today, most managers believe people working in the system, not the system itself, are the primary cause of errors and failures. While people working in the system can quickly spot the problems, managers seldom see anything wrong with the systems they've created. When problems occur, managers are quick to conclude that the workers, not the systems they've created, have failed. Whether they intend to or not, managers use the system to bully employees into compliance. Even those employees who initially question the system eventually give in.

There are Systems Thinkers like W. Edwards Deming (considered by many to be the father of the modern quality movement) who have pointed out that people are not what causes failures in a system.

On the contrary, the failures are caused by the design of the system. Deming proved that rather than reducing failures, "fixes" imposed from the top frequently *increase* them. He pointed out that those at the top, because they don't work on the front lines where they can directly observe problems, can't see the design flaws of the systems and therefore correct them. As a result, the systems they create are often wasteful, create barriers to quality, and are unresponsive to variation in customer demand.

An *Own It Culture*, however, makes the people who work within the systems responsible for improving the systems, by continuously experimenting with improving workflow and removing waste. People on the frontlines working in the systems, who are able to directly observe problems are expected to take responsibility for correcting the flaws.

Managers and supervisors take on the role of facilitators, teachers, coordinators and partners in the system improvement process.

In most organizations, the processes look something like this:

- An individual worker, a department, or other functional group receives an input (this could be an order, paperwork, a service, raw material, etc.).
- A series of activities is performed (that theoretically add value).
- An output is created (to another individual, department, or group within the organization or to a customer.)

This process works fine, as long as there are no problems and as long as customers are willing to accept the products and services as offered. However, often problems do occur, and customers often want some kind of accommodation. The annoying thing about customers is that they want what they want, exactly the way they want it, which often is not what the process is designed to produce.

Workers who try to respond to what customers want, find that their hands are tied. In effect, team member who try to accommodate customers are forced to choose to either please their customer or please their boss.

Since mid-level managers in conventional organizations are the "keepers of the processes," employees are not allowed to address process problems, even when they're aware of problems and might have a solution. It places team members in a dilemma: if they challenge the process or try to work around obvious flaws, they may be reprimanded, and if they stick to a way of doing business they know doesn't work, they'll be unable to deliver a good result for their customers. Eventually they become frustrated and disengaged.

As former CEO of the energy giant, AES, Dennis Bakke puts it, "We have made the workplace a frustrating and joyless place where people do what they're told and have few ways to participate in decisions or fully use their talents."[19]

It's not that the managers, who are keepers of the processes, don't care about the people that labor within them or their customers. Of course they do. After all, without loyal customers and hardworking energetic employees, no organization can stay in business. But rigid processes don't allow enough flexibility for people to take responsibility for responding to variations in what customers want and need.

Connecting People to Resources

One of primary objectives within the *Own It Culture* is to set up an environment where individuals learn how to solve problems independently and are equipped to do so. As this empowerment process happens, team members begin seeking the resources necessary to solve problems. As an Emergent Leader, it becomes our responsibility to assist these team members to connect to the resources they need. There are typically four types of resources needed: information, time, money, and talent.

More Information

There's an old saying that "information is power." This is because in conventional top-down cultures, the usual beliefs are that information should be shared only on a "need-to-know" basis, and all information should be considered confidential unless otherwise indicated. Why is information treated as confidential? Because, by controlling the flow of information, those at the top feel they're better able to directly control both activity and results.

By limiting access to information, conventional leaders become the sole conduit through which all information flows; information is shared downward only with their explicit approval. Since information is often used to assign blame and give out punishment, sharing the truth becomes dangerous. As a result, people up and down the chain of command will often tell their bosses what they want to hear. They'll manipulate the numbers in reports in order to avoid being blamed for bad news.

In contrast to this, in an *Own It Culture*, information is available to anyone who needs it. The rule of thumb is "no secrets" unless the information, for reasons of safety, security and legality, needs to remain confidential. By allowing information to flow freely, workers are able to solve problems, improve workflow, remove roadblocks, and respond to variations in customer demand quickly and efficiently without having to wait for approval.

People in An *Own It Culture* have access to two broad categories of information: *tactical information* needed for day-to-day tasks, and *strategic information* that provides the context for longer-term decision making and problem solving. Strategic information allows people to "see the big picture", so that they understand how the work they're doing contributes to the organization's broader purpose.

Just making information available is not enough. Information must flow freely. To illustrate, a study conducted by General Motors (GM) provides us with insights into how differently GM and Toyota viewed the role of team leaders and how that impacts the flow of information:

- Team Leaders at GM reported they spent only 52% of their time doing work on the shop floor, while team leaders at one of the Toyota plants spend 90% of their time directly involved with work on the shop floor. (Impact: Communicating what is going on is difficult if your team leader is gone half the time.)
- 21% of the team leader's time at Toyota was spent filling in for workers who were absent or on vacation. Whereas GM leaders only did this 1.5% of the time. (Impact: By filling in for front-line workers more often, team leaders pick up a lot more information about how well the system is working more because they're observing the work firsthand.)
- 10% of Toyota's team leader's time was spent ensuring a smooth flow of parts to the line. GM team leaders were only 3%. (Impact: Team leaders at Toyota are much more aware of inaccuracies of information that might affect getting the right parts to the line on time.)
- 7% of the Toyota team leader's time was spent actively communicating job-related information. This was virtually absent at GM. (Impact: Front-line workers are much more aware of what's going on throughout the plant and with changes in customer demand.)
- 5% of the Toyota team leader's time was spent observing the team working, in order to anticipate problems. This did not happen at all at GM.[20] (Impact: By directly observing the team working, supervisors at Toyota have unfiltered information about workflow, and as a result, are able to make adjustments before problems occur.)

Even though GM was trying to implement Toyota management concepts, they clearly had failed to understand the team leader's role in enhancing the flow of information. Whereas Toyota has made their team leaders partners with workers on the floor, sharing in the work, helping the workers anticipate problems and improve workflow, and otherwise communicating job-related information.

More Time

In a fast-paced world where the pressure to perform accelerates daily, workers at every level of an organization feel the pressure to meet deadlines, complete projects, fulfill production quotas, and improve the systems. Yet, according to a survey published on Salary. com, "The average worker admits to frittering away 2.09 hours per 8-hour workday, not including lunch and scheduled break-time." [21]

If it's true that the average worker wastes more than a quarter of their time each day, what are they really saying when they ask for more time? In many cases, they're really asking to be relieved of tasks which they see little or no value in. Ask workers in a conventional top-down culture whether much of what they do is a waste of time (as dictated by their job descriptions or the systems they work in) and they'll tell you, "Absolutely... but that's management's fault!"

Placed in an *Own It Culture*, however, these same workers are able to find the time they need by removing roadblocks and improving workflow. In short, they eliminate time-wasting tasks. In many cases, finding the time needed to solve a problem or complete a project is simply a matter of reordering priorities and putting less important tasks aside.

An Emergent Leader may help co-workers find more time by filling in for them while they continue working on an important project that takes them away from their normal job duties.

At times, however, finding more time may require a temporary change in a worker's job responsibilities. In this case, workers may need to negotiate with their colleagues. That is, workers may need to convince their co-workers who may not be as busy to take on some of their current job duties until they're able to complete the project or solve the problem. In an *Own It Culture*, this kind of give-and-take of job responsibilities happens all the time. This strategy tends to eliminate workers frittering away time by encouraging them to help out co-workers who are overloaded, knowing that they can expect the same help when they become busy.

More Money

In an *Own It Culture*, discussions about allocating more money for solving problems are not about offering an incentive, a pay increase, or a bonus. Money discussions are more likely to be about additional funds for operating/capital budgets. While the old saying "You can't solve a problem by simply throwing money at it" is true, of course, it could be that adding money to the budget may be justified — provided that a solid business case for the request can be made for the additional funds.

Of course, no organization has unlimited funds and every organization is concerned about the wise allocation of financial resources. In an *Own It Culture*, Emergent Leaders step forward to help co-workers seeking resources to develop and present a business case explaining how the added expenditure will benefit customers and the organization.

A business case may, or may not, be a formal written proposal. Regardless of the form of the proposal, a request for additional funds should be submitted to the appropriate forum within the organization for approval. This might be to the leadership group within the team, or for larger expenditure, to the organization's Senior Executive Team.

Tom Peters, the well-known author and management consultant, tells the story of a worker on the frontline at Harley-Davidson who made a proposal to purchase a major piece of equipment for the shop floor. Being accustomed to seeing top-down environments where ideas come exclusively from the top, Peters was astonished to overhear the staff member telling a co-worker that he's sweating over a proposal.

There was a staff member who had talked to vendors, run the numbers, and put together a business case for making a capital expenditure. Unlike conventional cultures where workers are told by management, "You don't get paid to think; now get back to work!" – workers at Harley-Davidson routinely develop business cases for making changes they'd like to implement.[22]

Anticipating the occasional need for additional operating funds, some organizations pre-authorize a set amount of money that can be spent without prior approval. In some retail establishments, team member may be provided with a small budget of $500-$2,000 annually to appease unhappy customers. In this situation, the business case for the expenditure is made after the fact.

The main point regarding money as a resource is that everyone in an *Own It Culture* learns how to make a business case for additional funds, or to simply use good judgment when additional spending is needed. Most times, this can easily be handled by an individual or a small group of workers. At other times, developing a business case often requires the help of an Emergent Leader with financial skills and experience.

More Talent

"I need some help!" How often have we heard these words from a co-worker? Unfortunately, managers in conventional top-down cultures answer this cry for help by asking people to simply work harder. They try to improve productivity through short-term solutions such as demanding that people work longer hours and suspending vacation time. In the end, these productivity-boosting strategies, while perhaps achieving short-term cost savings, do not and cannot result in sustainable gains in productivity.

Experience has shown that people, when asked to work harder, may be able to increase their productivity for short periods of time. However, workers cannot sustain increased levels of productivity for an extended period without working smarter, improving processes and systems, or finding ways to eliminate waste.

Sometimes the volume of work simply exceeds the capacity of the people available for the tasks. At these times, shifting job responsibilities among the existing work force or asking team leaders to fill in is inadequate; more workers are required. In this case the question is: Who do we let in? Where do we find the right people who are skilled, self-motivated and trustworthy enough to get the job done?

If you ask managers in conventional top-down cultures, they will likely tell you that good people are rare, that most people are average at best, or are more likely to be poor performers. Their experience tells them they're right, because most managers in these cultures find that 90% of their people significantly under-perform compared to their "A players."

Interestingly, organizations that have established an *Own It Culture* seem to have no difficulty finding good people who thrive in a highly collaborative work environment.

Organizations that have successfully created an *Own It Culture* are able to, as Nordstrom management puts it, "achieve extraordinary results with ordinary people."[23] This is because the work environment is so radically different from conventional cultures. Organizations that believe in people taking responsibility screen for character first, skill and experience second. They look for and hire people who are values-driven, self-motivated, and are willing to take responsibility.

Systems Thinking with a Twist

Through my years of partnering with leaders to drive change and bring to life an *Own It Culture*, one of the most consistent challenges is the 'system'. Whether we're talking about a system or a process or the way decisions are made, what I'm referencing is the toolbox we put in the hands of our team members to get the job done.

Leaders of an *Own It Culture* build flexibility into the processes by maximizing the ability of team members to respond to the unique needs and desires of each individual customer. Since the keystone of an *Own It Culture* places the needs of customers in a central role, a new operational model is called for. It's a model where team members on the frontlines take the primary responsibility for delivering an incredible customer experience and deliver on the value desired by the customer. We accomplish this by using *Systems Thinking with a Twist*.

Systems Thinking is a framework that is based on the belief that the only way to fully understand why problems in any system persist, is to understand the part in relation to the whole. Systems Thinking asserts that the conventional approach of focusing on solving individual problems without understanding how the design of the system causes or contributes to these problems often exacerbates them. This is based on the belief that the component parts of a system will act differently when the system's relationships are removed and each part is viewed in isolation.

The twist is we always view an organization's systems and processes from a dual vantage point. In the *Own It Culture*, leaders must view the organization's system and processes (the toolbox) from two points of view. First, team members must have the systems and processes in place to support the work needing to be done. In other words, are the tools we have put in team members hands making the work harder or easier for them to complete?

Then from a second view, from the customer side of things, do the systems and processes that the customer interacts with actually help them engage with the organization, get what they need and the outcome they hoped for, in a way that felt fantastic leaving them wanting more?

By adding the twist of viewing systems from the customer's point of view, we cause the designers of the organizations toolbox to build flexibility into the systems and maximize the ability of people working within the systems to respond to variations in customer demand.

We will dive deeper into how to put the necessary *System Thinking* practices into place in the Chapter on "Delivering Customer Value" later in this book. In the meantime, I encourage you to recognize the importance of the toolbox as being essential to assembling the right resources in the *Own It Culture*.

CHAPTER 6

Own It: Coaching for Success

"

*A desk is a dangerous
place from which to
view the world."
– John le Carré*

In a world where the pace of change is accelerating, where new ideas, new products and new ways of doing things has become the norm, expanding your knowledge and skills is essential. Books, articles, on-line resources, and classroom instruction are all effective avenues toward learning.

In spite of these helpful sources, when you're on the job, there is no substitute for finding a good coach: someone who not only already possesses knowledge, skills and experience, but someone who's able to effectively transfer this information to others in a way that others can understand and act on it.

To illustrate this, let me share another personal story.

I started this book by sharing my golf adventures. Several years ago, I was inspired to take up the game of golf. Although the pros I watched on TV could blast the ball 300 yards down the center of the fairway with relative ease, chip onto the green with deadly accuracy, and sink puts from several feet away, I found all of these seemingly simple skills incredibly difficult to master.

I tried learning the game by subscribing to a popular golf magazine, hitting hundreds of balls at the practice range, and playing as often as I could on a little "executive" course, (which simply refers to being shorter and supposedly easier to master) near my home. Still, after months of trying to learn on my own, not only was I not improving, but my game was actually getting _worse_. As I now like to joke, I wanted to learn to play golf in the worst way, and by trying to teach myself I got my wish.

Trying to teach yourself is not always the best strategy.

Finally, I realized that I needed some coaching, so I drove out to a nearby public course and signed up for some private lessons. To my dismay, I found that I had acquired a number of very bad swing habits. I expected my coach to tell me it was hopeless. Instead, over the next several weeks, he patiently helped me improve my golf swing. At each lesson, we focused on just one small adjustment.

Scott isn't an effective coach just because he's a fine golfer (which he is) but the reason he is effective is because he possesses the coaching skills to transfer his knowledge of how to hit a golf ball to others. He often uses what we at *Fired Up! Culture* call: "The More and Less Coaching Model", which I will dive deeper into later in this chapter.

Creating Stewards of the Work

Peter Block, the highly respected author and consultant, describes stewardship as, "The willingness to be accountable for the well-being of the larger organization."[24] In an *Own It Culture*, front-line workers are responsible for delivering customer value by both owning their jobs and owning the systems they work in. Emergent Leaders partner with co-workers as stewards of the systems. Although stewards are most often not literally owners of the business, they think and act like owners.

Job Ownership

Perhaps the best example I've come across of a CEO who has completely turned over ownership of individual jobs to team members is Ricardo Semler of Brazil-based *Semco*. Semler gives people the freedom to choose what they'd like to do, the right to decide on their personal working hours, and even the authority to set their own salaries.

Hard to believe? In doing business this way, Semco grew from $35 million in annual revenue, to $212 million in just six years. With more than 3,000 employees, they have virtually no staff turnover. Semler's philosophy of putting employee freedom and job satisfaction ahead of corporate goals has proven that it's possible to achieve incredible growth and profit that far exceed that of their competitors.

Consider the story of Auro Alves as told by Semler himself. "Auro Alves is a sales and technical-assistance manager at Semco. He began his career with us as a truck driver. He'd driven a bus in São Paulo before joining Semco and expected that he'd spend his life as a heavy-duty commercial driver. Less than five months after coming to Semco, he moved into product acquisition, and eight months after that, took a job as a junior buyer. He got involved in union activities, (that's right, Semco is a *union* organization) discovered that he liked being a leader, and that other workers were comfortable with his management style, too. He had a knack for coming up with new ways of doing old tasks at Semco in order to involve more people.

"While at Semco, Auro has taken dozens of elective courses, including English, Spanish, computer, negotiation technique, sales methods, and customer care. He's had offers to work elsewhere but turned them down because Semco allows him to grow. Auro isn't finished exploiting his own 'reservoir of talent.' He has a five-year plan of his own, even if the company frowns on them for itself. He owns a beach house in Peru and spends part of his seven-day weekend there fishing and getting to know the local people. (*Seven-Day Weekend* is the title of one of Semler's book.) He plans to move there one day and run his own 'virtual business' as a supplier or consultant to Semco."

At Semco, people like Auro are not only encouraged to develop their own job skills and to explore different job opportunities within the organization; they even determine their own salaries. There are no set salary systems within the company. Rather, each self-managed group decides what makes the most sense for them. This might include "fixed salaries, bonuses, profit sharing, commissions, royalties on sales, royalties on profits, commissions on gross margin, stock or stock options, Initial Public Offering (IPO) or sales."

They allow groups to set their own salaries based on five factors: (1) external wage comparison survey data, (2) internal wage comparison data, (3) the market conditions that determine whether they can pay above or below the market, (4) what each individual would like to be making, and (5) what their spouses, neighbors and friends are making.

Of course, the last two factors are known only to each individual. The others are made known to the company employees. By making the first three factors known to employees, an *Own It Culture* makes each individual responsible for justifying their salary to co-workers.

"Anyone who requests too large a salary or too big a raise runs the risk of being rejected by their fellow stewards – their colleagues. So, not too many people ask for excessive paychecks." Semler concludes his argument for allowing people to set their own salaries by saying, "If workers understand the big picture, they'll know how their salaries fit into it." [25]

CEOs like Ricardo Semler and other organizations that have created an *Own It Culture* support job ownership because they understand how much taking this approach benefits both customers and the organization. Customers are happier because they're interacting with team member who, because they own their jobs, are willing and able to do what it takes to meet their unique needs. The executives of the company are happier because the company operates with far less waste and much better profitability.

Professional Growth Mindset

In order to successfully link responsibility with accountability, it's important that people have the freedom to explore, that is, to choose the tasks they're willing and able to take on. It's the element of choice that allows them to take on more responsibility. In an *Own It Culture*, people are given the freedom to negotiate with their co-workers to exchange or share job responsibilities.

As the word implies, negotiating requires some give and take among the participants. This means that no one in the group is given the right to cherry-pick the best tasks leaving the worst chores to others. It also means that someone called a "boss" no longer assigns or delegates job tasks either. Instead, members in an *Own It Culture* decide together who will be responsible for each task.

The process works something like this:

- First, the team reaches agreement on their reason for existence (purpose), who their customers are, and what their customers need and want.
- Next, they list all of the important tasks which the team is responsible and accountable for.
- Then, they begin negotiating who in the group is willing and able to take on each task, including those responsibilities that might traditionally have been given to a supervisor (things like planning, setting priorities and policies, and deciding who will do what each day).

Negotiating job tasks is a dynamic process. The team member who does each job task changes over time as people gain the experience and knowledge that they need to take on greater levels of responsibility and accountability. Other important negotiating issues include deciding how removing roadblocks and improving workflow will be done, how progress will be reported, to whom and how frequently, as well as how to keep the focus on delivering what customers value.

The goals of the job negotiation process are to:

1. Allow people to choose job responsibilities that are personally motivating.

2. Allow every person to become self-managing.

3. Make sure that every member of the team understands exactly what they have agreed to be responsible for, and who they're accountable to.

One of the goals of creating an *Own It Culture* is to give people the opportunity to rediscover a level of job satisfaction that they may have lost in a more conventional "managed" work environment. Giving people a high degree of control over their work lives is enormously important in reigniting full engagement in the jobs they've chosen. Although it may seem contradictory, in order for people to perform well in meeting the needs of customers, they need to be able to pursue their own self interests. They need to be allowed to do work that they find personally motivating and satisfying.

Put simply, people who feel trusted to pursue their own dreams, put their hearts and souls into their work.

Challenge the Assumptions about Coaching

In conventional top-down work cultures, coaching is something quite different from my experience in an *Own It Culture*. This is because in conventional cultures, some would refer to it as 'old school', coaches are operating under a different set of assumptions. Let's compare these assumptions across the two very different types of workplace cultures.

Old School Coaching Assumption: It's the boss's job to provide most of the coaching.

Emergent Leader's Coaching Actions: It's everyone's job to offer coaching whenever they spot a person in a "teachable moment." It's also everyone's job to seek out coaching whenever they need help learning or mastering a new skill.

In conventional business cultures, such as in sports, coaches are in a position of power. Because most sports coaches are working with developing athletes who are young people striving to master their sport, coaches are authority figures. The coach plans and runs practices, choose who plays and who doesn't, and in many sports, provides instruction and direction during the course of competition itself.

Coaches in conventional business cultures are also authority figures. They write the business plans, manage operations, choose which workers get the good assignments and which don't, and provide direction on a day-to-day or perhaps hour-to-hour basis. If there is coaching to be done, they do it.

In an *Own It Culture*, being a coach is not limited to people in a position of authority. Rather, coaching can be offered by anyone with knowledge and skills that will benefit others who are in a "teachable moment." A teachable moment is that moment when you're ready to be receptive to coaching; ready to hear and act on the information and direction a coach can provide.

The best way to alert a potential coach that you're at a teachable moment is to simply ask for coaching when you need it. To not ask for coaching when you really need it is a major violation in an *Own It Culture*.

Emergent Leaders learn to look for and respond to co-workers who indicate that they've reached a teachable moment. As illustrated in Ricardo Semler's story about his leadership workshops, Emergent Leaders tend to emerge in a group when it's struggling with a challenging new task. As frustration begins to become evident, or as the group appears to be struggling, an Emergent Leader often emerges to coach the group.

Old School Coaching Assumption: The boss's coaching is the most accurate and useful.

Emergent Leader's Coaching Actions: Accurate and useful coaching is available from virtually anyone.

In conventional organizations, one of the common assumptions of a boss is that they have the most skill and knowledge of anyone in the work group; and therefore, the boss's coaching must be the most accurate and useful for people on the front lines.

In fact, superior knowledge and skill are frequently the primary criteria for being promoted in a conventional top-down culture. Not so much in an *Own It Culture* where useful coaching is available from virtually anyone who possesses the knowledge you lack and the coaching skills to pass them along to you.

While a leader in an *Own It Culture* may possess superior knowledge and job skills, it's much more important that they possess the leadership skills necessary to effectively coach. In fact, in an *Own It Culture*, one of the most highly valued leadership responsibilities that the organization looks for in aspiring leaders is exceptional coaching skills.

Old School Coaching Assumption: It's the boss's job to improve individual performance and coach during formal performance appraisals.

Emergent Leader's Coaching Actions: Formal performance appraisals, because they usually happen infrequently, tend to have a negative impact on individual performance. In order for coaching to be effective, it must be provided immediately at a teachable moment.

In a culture where the belief is that one of a manager's or supervisor's main jobs is to assess and appraise the work output of subordinates, formal performance appraisals are considered a key tool. The focus is on evaluating individual performance, as well as the performance of each business unit.

In some organizations, someone other than a direct supervisor, like a co-worker or internal customer, appraises performance. The purpose of a performance appraisal may be to decide on promotions or raises, to assist in career development, to set and measure goals, and to provide other kinds of performance feedback.

Unfortunately, there is significant evidence that performance appraisals don't work. As Tom Coens and Mary Jenkins, authors of *Abolishing Performance Appraisals* put it, "Due to its inherent design flaws, appraisals produce distorted and unreliable data about the contribution of employees. Consequently, the resulting documentation is not useful for staffing decisions and often does not hold up in court. Too often, appraisal destroys human spirit and, in the span of a 30-minute meeting, can transform a vibrant, highly committed employee into a demoralized, indifferent wallflower who reads the want ads on the weekend."[26]

This conclusion is based on more than 50 years of academic studies, industry surveys and professional articles.

However, feedback offered without judgment can be very useful, provided the person receiving the feedback initiates it and has complete control of the feedback received, and complete freedom to make use of the feedback in any way they choose. In an *Own It Culture*, everyone is encouraged to take responsibility for getting feedback that will best serve their specific needs and situation.

Old School Coaching Assumption: The boss's main purpose for coaching is to motivate people to improve.

Emergent Leader's Coaching Actions: People must find their own motivation to improve. When people ask for coaching, they're already motivated and ready to learn and grow.

In conventional cultures, the assumption has been that it's the boss's job to motivate people to improve, as if people not in positions of leadership are somehow lacking a desire to improve. Once again, current research shows that the key to individual motivation lies not in "extrinsic" rewards like money and recognition. It lies in the "intrinsic" rewards like pride in a job well done and a sense that you're really making a difference.

In an *Own It Culture*, people decide for themselves when they're ready to learn and grow, and ready to ask for coaching. This form of self-management is a key component of intrinsic motivation. Part of being accountable is becoming very aware of your need to learn, and to take the initiative to ask for coaching.

Old School Coaching Assumption: The boss should offer coaching to help people address their weaknesses.

Emergent Leader's Coaching Actions: Coaching people on how to address their weaknesses does little to improve performance; building on a person's strengths is a much more effective coaching strategy.

Emergent Leaders understand intuitively that asking people to address their weaknesses does little to improve their performance. This is because, in most cases, these "weaknesses" stem from either a lack of natural aptitude, or a lack of interest in acquiring or improving a particular skill. If someone lacks the natural talent or aptitude for a skill, their efforts to improve will likely prove fruitless no matter how much effort is put into it. Likewise, coaching a person with low aptitude often proves to be a waste of time and energy for the coach.

A lack of interest in learning or improving a skill can show up for a number of reasons. It's possible that the individual may be bored with the activity and thinks that improving their skills will do little to relieve the boredom. It's also possible that the individual recognizes their lack of aptitude for the skill, and therefore expects very little improvement from investing additional time and effort.

A much better strategy is to build on a person's strengths, on their natural talents and interests. People are much more likely to invest great effort in activities that they believe will yield rewarding results.

Apply the Emergent Leader Coaching Guidelines

As I've already explained, Emergent Leaders look for a "teachable moment" before offering to coach. That's the moment when someone appears to be ready and receptive to coaching. Often this occurs after someone has struggled a bit with a new task or skill and has either stalled or is beginning to show some level of frustration.

While allowing someone to struggle a bit before offering coaching is generally a good idea, an Emergent Leader is sensitive enough to make the offer to coach before a co-worker is ready to give up. Teachable moments are very individual; they're unique to each person. Some people are very open to coaching, others may be overly dependent on their coach, and some may even be very resistant to coaching, even when they're struggling.

Asking permission with a question like, "May I offer you some advice?" shows respect for the person. Asking for permission before beginning to coach/help gives the person who appears to be at a teachable moment the element of control. This allows that person to choose whether or not they're ready or receptive to coaching. When offering to coach, Emergent Leaders do so as a friend and colleague, rather than as an authority figure (even if the coach is a person in authority.) The objective is to avoid any resistance to authority or resistance because of embarrassment or insecurity.

Emergent Leaders are willing to coach anyone who asks for help, regardless of title, rank or role. The focus is on providing coaching that will help the other person improve their skills and proficiencies.

Emergent Leaders are also willing to ask for coaching whenever they need help themselves.

Every person in an organization, even the most experienced among us, can learn from co-workers. Even when your training and experience are high, sometimes the coaching of another Emergent Leader is helpful simply because their point of view differs from your own. This is particularly true when it comes to how to best work with other teammates or customers who we may be having trouble relating to.

There's simply no one "best way" to deal with people; sometimes we benefit from being open to coaching from others on how to improve interpersonal exchanges. We need to be open to coaching from anyone who offers to help without becoming defensive. The key is to listen and act on coaching tips with a willingness to learn.

Coaching Corner

The Emergent Leader Coaching Guidelines

Guidelines for Coaching

- Look for a coachable moment before offering to coach.

- Ask for permission before beginning to coach.

- Offer coaching as a colleague, not as a superior.

- Be willing to coach anyone who asks for help.

Guidelines for Being Coached

- Ask for coaching whenever you need help.

- Be open to coaching from anyone who offers to help without becoming defensive.

- Listen to and act on coaching tips with a willingness to learn.

- Give your coach feedback by asking clarifying questions.

The Transformational Leadership Coaching (TLC) Method™

Heather graduated from her college in Boston with a degree in management. Even before she graduated from college, she began testing her management skills for an exclusive downtown spa, an upscale florist, and a music software company. When she moved cross-country to San Francisco, she transformed her experience into good-paying jobs and eventually became the manager of a full-service spa, which now employs about 30 people.

Since beginning her management career, Heather has rarely hesitated to pick up the phone and call her mentor, Beth. Heather and Beth have been partners in problem solving by talking through Heather's issues together and discussing her alternatives, weighing the pros and cons of each option. Beth avoids giving Heather advice. Rather, she spends a good deal of time asking questions, listening, and reflecting what she hears. This allows Heather the freedom to choose her own solutions and to take responsibility for the outcome of her decisions.

When you have skills and knowledge that might benefit others, it's important to look for mentoring opportunities. Yet, because mentoring requires a long-term commitment, it's equally important to enter into mentoring relationships carefully, asking permission to mentor and offering to mentor as a partner, not as a person in authority. Likewise, when seeking a mentor, choose someone who shows a willingness to put your interests ahead of their own. Look for someone who has the time to mentor and is clear about what they have to contribute to the relationship and who will treat you as a peer.

Like Heather's mentor, Beth, a good coach employs a number of subtle skills including listening, asking questions, and providing feedback.

The *Four-Step Transformational Leadership Coaching Method*™ provides you with a good model for doing all of these. Step 1: Discovery, Step 2: Coaching, Step: Debriefing, and Step 4: Accountability.

THE FOUR STEP
TLC METHOD

DISCOVERY

Open-Ended Questions: "What is the problem as you see it, Heather?"

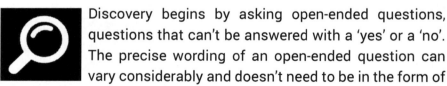

Discovery begins by asking open-ended questions, questions that can't be answered with a 'yes' or a 'no'. The precise wording of an open-ended question can vary considerably and doesn't need to be in the form of a question, as long as it gets Heather talking about her issue or problem.

For example, Beth might say, "Tell me what happened." Beth might follow up with other open-ended questions like: "So, how do you think your co-worker would describe this problem?" or "Is there another way to look at this problem?"

Restating: "Heather, I hear you saying..."

Periodically restating accomplishes a number of purposes. First, restating reassures Heather that she is being heard, which encourages her to continue talking. Second, it gives Heather an opportunity to correct and clarify Beth's restatements. Third, restating, like looking into a mirror, helps Heather reflect on and clarify her thoughts and feelings. Fourth, restating is a wonderful tool for helping Heather when she may be rambling or caught up in emotions; it helps her to refocus and get back on track.

Of course, if Beth over-uses restatement as a tool, she begins to sound like a parrot; or worse, gives Heather the impression that she's being ridiculed or belittled.

COACHING

Observations: "Heather, here's my take on the problem you've described..."

 During the coaching stage, Beth tries to make her observations as objective and non-judgmental as possible. Beth describes the problem as she sees it and gives an assessment of the magnitude and scope of each of the issues. Beth's observations might include how Heather might be contributing to the problem and other issues Heather might not have considered.

Coaching Conversation: "Heather, have you considered...?"

The goal of offering coaching is to help Heather find her own solution, not to offer a solution. It's not really important that the solution Heather chooses is, in Beth's opinion, a great solution or even a good solution. The important thing is that the solution might work. Once again, the key psychological element is: choice.

Studies have shown that average solutions, which are developed and implemented by the people working to solve a problem, outperform brilliant solutions developed by someone else.[27]   Part of human nature is that we take pride and ownership in our own creations and we're far less invested in the creations of others. Put another way: when Heather chooses how to solve a problem, she'll find a way to make it work.

DEBRIEFING

Next Steps: "So, now that we've talked the problem over, and we've discussed possible solutions, Heather, what are your next steps?"

 The idea, during the debriefing stage is to help Heather arrive at a specific course of action. Beth continues to ask "next step" questions until both Beth and Heather are clear about what to do and are both confident that the solution has a chance to work. Talking through next steps gives Heather the confidence to give the solution she's chosen a try. It may also be appropriate for Heather and Beth to agree on whether, and how, Heather might report back to Beth on the outcome of implementing her solution. Together, they can talk about lessons learned and/or possible additional next steps.

Coaching Feedback: "Was my advice helpful, Heather?"

Although the main focus of offering coaching is on helping Heather find a solution to her issue, it's also important for Beth to ask for some feedback on whether or not the counseling session was helpful, and if not, why not. Every person who offers counsel has a favorite style, one that fits their own personality and problem-solving process.

Beth's style and process may not meet Heather's needs completely. Heather may be looking more for emotional support (without directly asking for it) rather than specific problem-solving ideas. Beth may be distracted by the issue itself or may not pick up on subtle, non-verbal cues given by Heather. It would be a good idea for Beth to ask something like, "Heather, is there anything I could do differently that would be helpful the next time we talk about an issue?"

ACCOUNTABILITY

Check-ins: "Last week we discussed a couple of your challenges and you decided to take some action. Heather, how are things going? What's working for you? And what's not working?"

 The premise, during the accountability step, is to assist Heather to stay committed to follow through with the actions she has committed to doing. Beth continues to check in around the agreements and action list. This will keep everyone on track while at the same time providing the opportunity to work through issues that may have come up. It's not uncommon to find that the things discussed during the TLC coaching sessions are not as easily applied in real time. There often are variables that were simply not anticipated.

Course Correction: "Based on what's working and what's not, Heather, what do you see needing to change?"

Course correction accomplishes a number of purposes. Firstly, it ensures Heather remains on an active track. If something is not working, she needs to address it and not continue to do things blindly. Secondly, it gives Heather an opportunity to hold herself and Beth accountable to the actions and agreements that were made. Thirdly, revisiting things regularly prevents the coaching topics from getting buried in the busyness of life and work. Course correction as close to real-time is critically important.

The Heart of the TLC Method: Connected Values

Let's take a moment and revisit our *Connected Values Framework* and make the connection to an Emergent Leader applying the Transformational Leadership Coaching Method. It's here where the power of the models working together begin to really see the fruits in the workplace and bring the *Own It Culture* strategy to life.

Truth

Sharing the truth is not always easy. It's particularly difficult to share the truth when the truth is bad news or when there is genuine disagreement over what the truth really is. As human beings, we share an intense need to preserve our own sense of righteousness when something has gone wrong. That is, we don't want to admit or believe that we might be a cause in a problem or issue.

An Emergent Leader can be of great help in uncovering or sorting out "the truth" without resorting to scapegoating. As each player in the drama shares their version of the story, an Emergent Leader can help each person see that there may indeed be more than one valid version of the "truth." An Emergent Leader can also help the players explore and understand the feelings involved and to recognize that feelings are an important part of the truth.

Trust

Building and sustaining trust requires effective two-way communication. We extend trust to our co-workers by allowing them to choose to take on responsibilities and to carry out agreements and promises. When trusting others, we need to be clear about our expectations and courageous enough to ask for help when we need it. Yet, people often lack the courage to trust without the help of an Emergent Leader.

When communication breaks down, it often takes a third party, an Emergent Leader, to get communication flowing again and rebuild trust.

Honesty

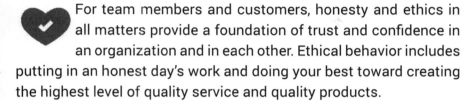 For team members and customers, honesty and ethics in all matters provide a foundation of trust and confidence in an organization and in each other. Ethical behavior includes putting in an honest day's work and doing your best toward creating the highest level of quality service and quality products.

Emergent Leaders often play the role of the conscience of an organization, challenging groups and individuals to examine their behaviors and actions to be sure that they're consistent with their stated values. In other words, that there is integrity between words and actions.

Respect

Greeting people on the street, in the store, at the gym, or even in the workplace, can seem like such a chore for some people. But what many people forget is that saying "good morning" isn't just being polite. By saying "good morning," one person is showing respect for another person, not just by greeting them, but by simply acknowledging that they exist.

In the workplace, over half of employees claim that they don't regularly get respect from their colleagues, and in particular, their leaders. This is especially notable since employees also report that being treated with respect by leaders is more important than any other leader behavior. Emergent Leaders show respect for others. Period. No exceptions. Whether actively listening to a colleague or cleaning up the office kitchen, showing respect for others in the workplace provides transformative benefits.

Mentoring

Mentoring is a great way to share knowledge and experience. Fortunately, it doesn't have to always be a one-way conversation, i.e., mentoring flowing from a senior, more experienced person to a protégé. Mentoring is available to everyone at every level of experience – from colleagues more experienced than us and from those who can offer us a fresh perspective, like new members of the organization and younger colleagues.

Mentoring is not the exclusive role of supervisors, managers and senior workers. In fact, a manager or supervisor might put a mentor and protégé together when the two might not have otherwise found each other.

Openness

Openness to new ideas is the key to improving workflow, to solving problems, and to meeting the unique needs of each customer. Frankly, openness is the primary component to innovation.

An Emergent Leader helps co-workers to be receptive to new ideas by examining their pre-conceived ideas and prejudices and opening them up to exploring new ideas and finding new solutions to old problems.

Courage

For an organization to remain dynamic and competitive in the marketplace, it needs people who have the courage to act on their beliefs and to step forward with new ideas, whether these ideas are popular or not.

Emergent Leaders are instrumental in helping to create a risk-taking environment, helping to establish an environment where new ideas can be brought forward and examined without prejudice and an environment where it's safe to challenge the status quo without fear of reprisal.

Giving Credit

All human beings have the need to be recognized and feel appreciated for what they contribute. Recognizing the contributions of co-workers will provide a foundation of fairness in the organization that helps fuel the fire of personal motivation. It helps keep people enthusiastically engaged in their work and with each other.

Emergent Leaders don't need to become cheerleaders in order to give credit where it is due. They can help this process by simply bringing individual and group contributions to light so that their efforts and results are acknowledged.

Selflessness

Selfless behavior may seem an unrealistic expectation in an organizational setting, particularly in conventional organizations where internal competition is common. The truth is that unless customers and colleagues feel that we're considering their needs and that we're putting their interests ahead of our own, they will cease to do business with us. Offering counsel is an act of selfless behavior.

Rather than giving advice or offering a solution, Emergent Leaders consider their own selfish needs and desires to be less important than the needs of those they work with. I.e., they prioritize other people's needs over their own needs.

Coaching Corner

Effective coaching begins by recognizing a teachable moment. Good coaches offer only one more tip and one less tip at a time, so that the person can process the information and put it into practice independently.

Emergent Leaders assume the following about coaching:

1. It's every person's job to offer coaching whenever they spot a person in a "teachable moment." It's also everyone's job to seek out coaching whenever they need help learning or mastering a new skill.

2. Accurate and useful coaching is available from virtually anyone.

3. Formal performance appraisals tend to have a negative impact on individual performance. In order for coaching to be effective, it must be provided without judgment at a teachable moment.

4. People must find their own motivation to improve; when people ask for coaching, they're already motivated and ready to learn and grow.

5. Coaching people on how to address their weaknesses does little to improve performance; building on a person's strengths is a much more effective coaching strategy.

COACHING ACTIONS

Recognize a teachable moment	Empathize with the learner	Make an offer to coach/help

I suggest *more* of …   I suggest *less* of …

The ***More and Less Coaching Model*™** is a process that begins by recognizing a teachable moment and continues until the person has mastered the new skill. Here's how a coaching session using the *More and Less Coaching Model*™ on the job might sound:

Bob: "Mary, it looks to me like you're really struggling with operating that machine. I can sure understand how you feel – most people new to that machine have struggled with it the first time they've tried to use it. If you'll allow me to help you, I have some ideas that I think might help you out."

Mary: "Well, Bob, I thought I was ready to handle this machine on my own after you and I worked together on it yesterday, but you're right, I'm having a tough time with it today. I'd sure appreciate your help."

Bob: "I'd be glad to help, Mary. Let me offer a couple of tips based on what I've observed just in the last few minutes since I stopped by to see how you were doing.

"Firstly, I'd suggest that you be a little less concerned about the number of units you're producing right now while you're still learning how to operate the machine. It will take a while before you'll be producing the same number of units as the experienced operators.

"Secondly, I suggest you spend a little more time making sure the new materials being added to the staging bin are lined up correctly. I think doing that should stop the machine from jamming. Why don't you give it a try right now?"

With Bob's help, Mary clears the jam and places the materials in the staging bin. She restarts the machine and carefully monitors the machine's output. After a few minutes she adds material to the staging bin, and the machine jams again.

Bob: "Mary, the machine was humming along just fine. What do you think happened?"

Mary: "I think it had something to do with the material I added to the staging bin."

Bob: "Right you are! Now what do you think needs to change?"

Mary: "Oh, I remember now! When I add material to the staging bin, I have to check that the leading edge of the material matches up perfectly with the material already in the bin, right?"

Bob: "Right again, Mary! Why don't you do that and let's see what happens."

Mary clears the jam, aligns the material in the staging bin and starts the machine again. Bob observes as Mary adds material to the staging bin three more times. She is careful to make sure that the leading edge of the new material matches up perfectly with the material already in the bin and no more jams occur.

Bob: "Looks like you've got it under control, Mary. I hope you found my coaching helpful. If you have any more trouble, call me on my cell, okay?"

Mary: "You've been a great help. I'll call if I get stuck again; and Bob, thanks!"

One piece of advice here — keep it simple and focused. It's important to note that the coach should offer no more than one "more of" and one "less of" tip at a time (a little more of this and little less of that). Many coaching sessions are unsuccessful because the coach gives the person being coached too much information all at once. To teach a complex task, a good coach breaks the coaching down into a series of small steps, each of which can be understood and acted on by the person being coached without confusion.

The *More and Less Coaching Model* allows the person being coached to process and practice each small step until they are successful. It also allows the coach to zero in on the specific areas where the person being coached needs the most practice. Of course, complex skills often require multiple coaching sessions, allowing the person being coached the time (often a day or more) to master the step they've learned before tackling the next step in the skill.

The true measure of a successful coaching session is a person who is able to understand and apply what they have learned, and to repeat the new skill successfully in the future independently.

SECTION 3:

DELIVERING ON THE CUSTOMER PROMISE

*"A community is like a ship; everyone ought
to be prepared to take the helm."*
– Henrik Johan Ibsen

In this Section:

- Linking Responsibility to Accountability
- Encouraging the Formation of Self-Managing Teams
- Delivering Customer Value in 'TransFormation Zones'
- The Ignite Change Method
- Rewriting the Ways of Management
- Expecting Everyone to Play

R alph Stayer, the third generation CEO of the successful family business, Johnsonville Foods, found himself worrying not just about the competition, but about what he perceived as "the gap between potential and performance." He observed, "Our people didn't seem to care. Every day I came to work and saw people so bored by their jobs that they made thoughtless, dumb mistakes. No one was deliberately wasting money, time, and materials; it was just that people took no responsibility for their work. They showed up in the morning, did half-heartedly what they were told to do, and then went home."

So, Stayer went to work to get to the bottom of the problem. After much soul searching, his first insight was that if there were problems, it was his fault, not his managers' and workers' fault. So, he set about trying to find a way to create an organization "where people took responsibility for their own work, for the product, for the company as a whole." Acting on instinct alone, he ordered change.

"From now on," he announced to his management team, "you're all responsible for making your own decisions." As he described it, "I went from authoritarian control to authoritarian abdication," and the results were a disaster. "After more than two years of working with them, I finally had to replace all three top managers."

From his early failures, he learned two important lessons. The first was, "I couldn't give responsibility. People had to expect it, want it, even demand it." The second lesson was realizing, "I didn't control the performance of the people at Johnsonville, that as a manager I didn't really manage people. They managed themselves. I did manage the context. The power of any contextual factor lies in its ability to shape the way people think and what they expect. So, I worked on two contextual areas: systems and structures."[28]

Authoritarianism has been the dominant organizational system and structure for centuries. Authoritarianism operates on the assumption that an elite class of individuals has the right to exercise power and control over others by virtue of accumulated wealth, superior intelligence, or position of authority. Paternalism, a close relative to authoritarianism, endows power to a patriarch or matriarch, who gives favors and protection in exchange for loyalty.

Both authoritarianism and paternalism operate on the belief that pursuit of self-interest is a primary human motivator. Authoritarian and paternalistic leaders, perhaps because they're pursuing their own self-interest, expect to see the same motivation in the people around them. As a result, they create a politically charged environment where people gain power and prestige by helping their superiors solidify their power base.

This means that there is a heavy price for most of the people who are not in power. As Patricia McLagan & Christo Nel, authors of *The Age or Participation* write, "In authoritarian systems, citizens, employees, and even customers are essentially subservient or – worse – disenfranchised and disempowered."[29]

In the 21st century, a number of powerful forces are changing the way business and governmental organizations think about leadership systems and structures. Whereas in the past, authoritarian and paternalistic systems controlled the dissemination of information, with the rapid growth of the Internet and multiple media outlets, information is much more widely available. This makes it far easier for people to make their own decisions and manage their own lives.

With intensifying global competition, guaranteed lifetime employment is becoming a thing of the past, and as a result, workers are demanding more control over their work lives. Globalization has also blurred the boundaries between nations and within organizations.

This has necessitated the creation of products and services that can easily flow across borders. Technology has significantly reduced the need for physical labor to produce products, and since individuals now have a much more significant impact on creating value for customers, worker's commitment and involvement is more critical than ever to the survival of a business.

Customers have gained much greater control over the marketplace. Before World War II, business leaders like Henry Ford could get away with saying, "You can have a Ford in any color you like, as long as it's black."

Today, customers have lots of choices; they can shop around. They can decide the kinds of products and services they would like. Put bluntly, organizations that encourage every employee to take responsibility for delivering customer value are surviving. Those that have not, are not surviving.

CHAPTER 7

Own It: Linking Responsibility to Accountability

"

Vision comes alive when everyone sees where his or her contribution makes a difference."
– Ken Blanchard

Nathaniel Branden, Ph.D., the father of the self-esteem movement, describes 'self- responsibility' this way: "The practice of self-responsibility begins with the recognition that I am ultimately responsible for my own existence; that no one else is here on earth to serve me, take care of me, or fill my needs."[30]

Delivering on the customer promise depends on each member of the organization being self-responsible, recognizing that no one else in the organization exists to serve their needs; rather, they are responsible to the team, to the organization, and most importantly, to their customers. However, in order to consistently deliver customer value, responsibility must be linked to accountability.

The terms responsibility and accountability are often used interchangeably. In our practice, these two words seems to show up daily. While these two words are strongly related, they have distinctly separate meanings in an *Own It Culture*. Let's define responsibility and accountability in this context, and then clarify how responsibility and accountability are linked.

> **Responsibilities:** Tasks, duties, jobs and activities belonging to an individual or group.

> **Accountabilities:** Results that an individual or group has agreed or promised to deliver to customers, colleagues, and the organization.

Responsibility for individuals living and working in an *Own It Culture* begins with the freedom to make choices. Of course, choosing to take on any responsibility requires at least a minimum level of competence for the task. In self-managing teams, taking on responsibility also requires that individuals possess the skills to own their job without the need for supervision. Accountability to customers, to peers, and to the organization means that individuals working in self-managing teams are willing to deliver results, and when things go wrong, make it right.

The key differentiator between conventional hierarchical systems of accountability and how accountability shows up in an *Own It Culture* is the link between responsibility and accountability. Under conventional top-down models, responsibility and accountability are purposely separated. This means that responsibilities are assigned or delegated downward (through the chain of command), but at the end of the day, the person who delegated the task is accountable for the results (to a person of higher authority.)

People in authority take the blame (although they often try to pass the blame along) for the problems and failures and are held accountable for them.

One of the unintended negative outcomes of this separation of responsibility and accountability is that inevitably a great deal of effort is expended on finding the person or people who are accountable for problems and failures without looking, as Deming would advise, at the design of the system.

This became evident when the American public asked how torture and prisoner abuse could have occurred at Abu Ghraib prison. A few low-level soldiers were tried and convicted for these atrocities. They were characterized as "bad apples" and "rogues" acting on their own. On closer examination of the truth, it reveals that these soldiers were operating in a toxic system that, at the very least, failed to discourage such outrageous behavior, or at the very worst, encouraged it.

While these soldiers should be held accountable for their acts, it's more important that we challenge the operational philosophy that was responsible for creating such a toxic environment and hold the people further up the chain-of-command who created it accountable as well.

In contrast, in an *Own It Culture*, responsibility and accountability are intentionally linked. In other words, each person is responsible for the tasks they've chosen, and accountable for delivering those results. If something goes wrong, the person who chose to take on the task is responsible for making things right. Shifting blame upward or downward is not an option. "The buck stops here" is the responsibility-taking mantra for everyone.

At Nordstrom, the orientation and onboarding training makes a strong statement: "Employees are instructed to always make a decision that favors the customer before the company. They're never criticized for doing too much for a customer; they are criticized for doing too little."

One Nordstrom employee recalled a time when a customer, who was shopping in her department, realized that she had misplaced an earlier purchase of three bars of soap. "I went over to lingerie and got three more bars of soap and gave them to her. She thanked me and said, 'I can't believe you did this.' The bars of soap were only 90 cents each, but they produced a happy customer."[31]

The transformation to an *Own It Culture* at Harley-Davidson provides another example of an organization that came to understand, for the first time, the power of creating effective partnerships by establishing self-managing teams. Emerging from a period where the company nearly failed in the 1970s, during the 1980s, CEO Vaughn Beals launched a number of drastic changes. The first was reducing the workforce by 40% and cutting salaried employees' paychecks by 9%.

When the company continued to falter, they finally instituted a number of management-employee partnership initiatives.

As Rich Teerlink, Vaughn Beals' successor, put it, "We had to identify some sort of strategy that could carry everyone forward everyone meaning employees, customers, and all other stakeholders. We had to improve operations. And I felt strongly that we needed to change the way employees were being treated. They could no longer be privates, taking orders and operating within strict limits. We needed to continue to push, and push hard, to create a much more inclusive and collegial work atmosphere."[32]

So, under Beals' and then Teerlink's leadership, the management at Harley-Davidson partnered with their workers to craft a shared purpose of Harley's future. Workers were no longer to be treated as second-class citizens. They were encouraged to fully participate in system design and even had the right to say 'no' to proposed changes.

To pull this off, the participants had to establish absolute honesty between management and labor, systematically knocking down every barrier to quality they found. Management and labor partnered to design systems and structures that allowed them to be jointly accountable for delivering customer value and operational results.

By inviting workers on the frontlines of Harley-Davidson into the process of rethinking their systems, over time they were able to establish an effective partnership between labor and management that had not existed previously. Together, they created a system of responsibility that is the envy of industrial America today.

People working on the production line have taken full ownership of every part of the operation, from system design to quality control, and the results have been amazing. By setting up self-managing teams, they were able to rise out of the debt of the 1980s and become one of the most consistently profitable American manufacturers today, through good times and bad.

Like any company making the transition from conventional hierarchical management systems toward an Own It Culture, Harley's progress has not been without its challenges. Team member at

Harley-Davidson's largest manufacturing plant in York, PA were on strike for two weeks before reaching an agreement with management on wages and health care benefits.

This shows that even in organizations that have worked very hard at making the change to an *Own It Culture*, maintaining a healthy relationship between management and labor depends on maintaining a healthy social contract.

Encourage the Formation of Self-Managing Teams

In an *Own It Culture*, self-managing teams are responsible for designing systems capable of responding to the unique needs of their customers. People working together in self-managing teams fix workflow problems, increase or decrease production to match customer demand, and customize products and services specifically to meet the needs of each of their unique customers.

Members of self-managing teams take responsibility for every aspect of their operation. They design their own jobs, set their own workloads and schedules, and handle the finances, including setting budgets, planning capital expenditures and managing purchasing. They're also responsible for managing safety, maintenance and quality control, hiring and firing their own group members, and even deciding group member's compensation.

While serving as CEO of AES, Dennis Bakke encouraged the formation of Self-Managing Teams. In his book, *Joy at Work,* Bakke describes a visit he made to an AES power plant in Houston. While there, he sat in with a group that was modifying the employee handbook. As the group tried to account for every possible contingency, the handbook grew by several pages in less than an hour.

Frustrated by what he saw, Bakke asked the group a series of hypothetical questions: "What if we eliminated it [the handbook] altogether? What if we did away with procedure manuals? What if we did away with detailed job descriptions? What if we didn't have an organization chart with boxes representing people and their jobs? What if we didn't have any shift supervisors? What if there were no written limits on what individuals could authorize the company to spend? What if all the specialist titles given to employees were eliminated? What if we created teams of people around areas of the plant to operate and maintain the facility, instead of letting bosses assign tasks and run the plant? What if each team could set its own hours of work? What if team members hired and fired their own colleagues? What if you could make important decisions rather than leave them to your supervisor or the plant manager?"

The initial reaction to his questions upset the supervisors. In fact, the next day they were threatening to quit. After he calmed them down, he outlined his idea for what he called "Honeycomb" – an idea inspired by his beekeeper uncle.

Dennis explained that bees independently fly up to several miles from the hive collecting nectar before returning the hive. He used the analogy of a honeycomb to encourage workers at the Houston plant to "create an environment based on the same principles of trust, freedom, and individuals acting for the good of the larger team."

Two months later, he returned to the Houston plant and found that the workers had organized themselves into self-managing teams named after different types of bees ("e.g., mud daubers, hornets, wasps, and yellow jackets.") These teams became responsible for "budgets, workload, safety, schedules, maintenance, compensation, capital expenditures, purchasing, quality control, hiring, and most other aspects of their work life."

In this radical new approach of allowing people on the frontlines to manage and operate AES plants, a new kind of work environment was called for. It became an environment where workers at every level were trusted to make decisions for the good of all the stakeholders. This included the owners, certainly, but also the workers, the community the plant was located in, and the customers.

In this bold new environment, every worker was considered to be a "businessperson" who was responsible for maintaining resources (money, equipment, fuels) to meet the needs of all the stakeholders and of the community they operated in.

Since workers at every level were taking on so much responsibility and were becoming accountable to all stakeholders, Bakke insisted that these businesspeople should "ask for as much advice as possible before making a decision to ensure the best balance of interests possible among all the affected groups, without compromising the ultimate purpose of the company to meet a need in society."[33]

Ricardo Semler, CEO of Semco, has taken on the challenge of establishing self-managing teams throughout his company for a very practical reason. As he observes, "If humans are organized in a huge, complex group, they need complex regulations and procedures to govern them. If their organization is simplified, the way they're managed can be simplified, too. Best of all, they can manage themselves. If you want to know what time each of 40,000 employees arrive in the morning, you'll need a complex system of time clicks, cameras, penalties, and rewards. If you organize team member into groups of ten people each following a customized seven-day weekend [Semler's term for the workweek is: a seven-day weekend], those clusters can be counted on to monitor themselves. At Semco, our units [self-managing teams] are always a size that permits people to know each other, understand the whole picture, and negate the need for excessive control. At any rate, we usually organize along the lines of a half dozen to ten people who directly interact."[34]

Nordstrom has become the perpetual number one department store chain in the country by using self-managing teams to deliver outstanding service. Nordstrom team members are taught "The Nordstrom Way," which summarized briefly is "to provide outstanding customer service." Everyone in the organization understands that the specific products customers want can vary tremendously, while their expectation for outstanding customer service does not. To illustrate how well Nordstrom team members understand this point, here is a list of words and phrases a group of Nordstrom team member came up with when asked to think about customer service:

- Product Knowledge
- Courtesy
- Smiles
- Solution-Oriented
- Follow through
- Coordination
- Professionalism
- Find a need and fill it
- Don't make promises you can't keep
- Pleasing your customer

Whether you shop at a Nordstrom store or work there, it doesn't take long to see that there is a reason why Nordstrom has been historically successful while showing a great deal of resilience as markets, recessions and pandemics attack their business. The stores are organized into self-managing teams that focus on one thing: expecting every member of the organization to take responsibility for delivering extraordinary customer service.

TransFormation Zones: Delivering Value

Many organizations categorize customers by volume, profit margin or the type of product or service provided. For example, in the wholesaling business, customers are generally divided into three major customer types: "Customer Type A" for the highest volume customers, "Customer Type B" for mid-volume customers, and "Customer Type C" for low volume customers.

Typically, there are a small number of "A" customers accounting for a majority of their sales volume, so the wholesaler often allocates a small number of "A" customers to each sales team. Because there are typically a much larger number of "B" customers with moderate volume, the wholesaler will allocate more of these customers to each sales team. Finally, because the volume for "C" customers is so low, a large number of customers can be allocated to each sales team handling this category of customers.

TransFormation Zones move beyond this simple form of classification by sales volume to design systems that can respond to high levels of customer variation. Rather than asking customers to deal with each internal function separately (sales, service, administration, warehousing, etc.) people within each of these functions work together to create *TransFormation Zones* organized to serve the varying needs of their customers. *TransFormation Zones* don't replace functional groups; they bring them together to serve customers.

So, in a nutshell: *TransFormation Zones* are cross-functional teams that design systems and processes to give customers control of transactions. In other words, team members working together in *TransFormation Zones* design systems that are able to respond to preferences, requests, and yes, even the demands of each unique customer within a customer category. They fundamentally change a series of transactions or tasks to a *TransFormation* experience, where the 'wow' experience occurs and lasting loyal relationships are built.

Team members working in *TransFormation Zones* don't assume that customers who share a set of common metrics (such as sales volume or customer demographics) want the same things. Rather, they assume that what customers want now, in the future, will vary tremendously. So, they design systems in each *TransFormation Zone* that are capable of responding to this variation in what their customers want.

The primary goal of establishing *TransFormation Zones* is to deliver customer value by looking at the business from the customer's point of view. They start the process of forming *TransFormation Zones* by asking the following questions:

- How can we make it easy for our customers to do business with us?
- What is the best way for us to organize our TransFormation Zones to convenience our customers, rather than merely convenience ourselves?
- How do we ensure that every member of each *TransFormation Zone* has both responsibility and accountability for improving the system, and for delivering customer value?

Typically, a wholesaler's functions include sales, delivery, merchandising, warehousing, administration, and fleet maintenance. The sales, delivery and merchandising functions are organized into small teams that call separately on a group of common customers.

The warehousing group is divided into shifts. Administration and fleet maintenance operate as support functions to the rest of the system. While these functions must, to some degree, coordinate their efforts; for the most part, they operate independently of each other, trying to find the most efficient means of operation.

Organizing a wholesaler into *TransFormation Zones* looks like this. Cross-functional teams are formed that include each of their internal functions. These teams meet regularly to discuss the unique needs of the customers they serve, how their needs and expectations are changing, and how the systems and processes need to be modified to better meet these changing needs.

Since *TransFormation Zones* exist to serve the needs of each unique customer, they may be permanent, meaning they serve a long-term customer need. Members of *TransFormation Zones* design the systems and processes from the end of each process backward – the point where the customer receives the product or service – not from the beginning of the process forward as most organizations do.

Again, *TransFormation Zones* are designed so that customers drive the transactions, not the organization's policies and procedures. Customers decide what a quality *TransFormation Zone* looks like, they choose the precise products they want, and they select the level of service and support they need.

Disney theme parks understand the *TransFormation Zone* concept of allowing customers to drive the transaction very well. Disney does this by tapping into four elements of understanding its guests. This is what Disney calls "Guestology".

Guestology focuses on:

1. Needs
2. Wants
3. Stereotypes (expectations)
4. Emotions.[35]

In other words, guests at a Disney park are there because they <u>NEED</u> a vacation, they <u>WANT</u> lasting memories, they have very specific <u>STEREOTYPES</u> (expectations) of how the cast members should look (Mickey, Goofy, Donald, etc.), and they want to feel the EMOTIONS of excitement and fun.

For these reasons, Disney designs its parks so that guests can easily choose the specific activities that fulfill exactly what the guests want from their experience.

Disney has set up each of its theme parks to be an inter-connected web of *TransFormation Zones*. From the moment a guest passes through the ticket booth onto the grounds, the entire experience for the guests is designed to respond to their wants, needs, expectations, and emotions. From the layout of the park, to management of lines at each attraction, *cast members* (Disney's term for *all* park employees) do everything they can to make it easy for their guests to create their own memories.

Every cast member takes responsibility for removing any roadblocks that may hinder their guests' experiences. Together, they continue to innovate to find ways to improve the workflow in the park, so that they're delivering more of what their customers want.

When implemented across an entire organization, *TransFormation Zones* are scalable. That is, they can be formed at any time, for any customer and for any period of time. The number *TransFormation Zones* varies with the size of the organization, the types of products, services or solutions being provided, and the number of customer groups being served.

Making *TransFormation Zones* function well depends on encouraging every person working within each *TransFormation Zone* to take responsibility for tasks normally reserved for managers and supervisors in a conventional organization.

Giving Things a Boost

As we build out our *Own It Culture*, equip our team to self-manage and challenge them to identify and resolve issues, concerns and bottlenecks, as leaders we need to recognize that we're essentially unleashing change. For most, change is scary, challenging and disruptive. So how do we set up an environment for our people to navigate the necessary change? There are many theories and practices around change management, and this book is not intending to go deep into the practice of Change Management.

I would like to introduce you to two practices: the Boost Initiative and the Ignite Change Methodology. These practices can assist leaders in driving change in a way that supports the *Own It Culture* concepts.

Boost Initiatives™ is our methodology for studying real-life organizational issues or series of issues that, if properly addressed, resolved, or enhanced, would benefit the work team, the organization and the customers. The Boost Initiative is started to address a specific concern about a business issue. When implemented throughout an organization, Boost Initiatives are transformative in changing how the work is done, the experience of work for team members, and the results.

As part of the Boost Initiative conversation, I want to introduce you to our concept of a *TransFormation Team.* This team is made up of a small group of people who meet at regular intervals (at least every other week for an hour or more) to work on improving workflow and removing *TransFormation Blocks*.

Remember, *TransFormation Blocks* are anything that inhibit the customer transaction, disappoint the customer, slow the process, or cause other types of waste within the system.

When the scope of the project is narrow, that is, within a department, a *TransFormation Team* is drawn from members of the department. When the scope of the project is broad, that is, impacting multiple departments and/or customer groups, the membership of the *TransFormation Team* is multi-disciplinary.

Using the *Boost Initiatives™*, members of the *TransFormation Team* begin by studying the system from end to end. As they do so, they identify variation in the system, looking particularly for causes of failure demand.

Then, they plan a series of *Boost Initiatives*; and finally, they do the pilot and measure their results, looking for reductions in variation and removal of waste from the system. Their measures are carefully designed to help them better understand how the system works and, most importantly, to deliver more customer value.

The Ignite Change Method™

In our consulting work, my team and I have consulted with hundreds of organizations to drive change. Changes in thinking, strategy and execution. One of the most important methodologies in our change management toolkit is to help leadership embrace the *Ignite Change Method™*.

The *Ignite Change Method™* Framework follows the Systems Thinking approach of studying the system from end to end, identifying the causes of variation, failure and frustration, planning a series of pilot experiments, and measuring the results.

The *Ignite Change Method™* has four primary steps.

Step 1 – DISCOVERY
During the Discovery stage, questions are asked, assumptions are made, a theory is formed, and data is gathered.

Step 2 – DREAM
In the Dream stage, the vision of the system's new and improved output is formed.

Step 3 – DESIGN
In the Design stage, pilot programs are planned and the anticipated improvements are predicted.

Step 4 – DELIVER
In the Delivery stage, the experiments are conducted, results are measured to see whether the proposed improvements have actually improved the system in a way that enables the system to deliver better customer value.

One of the keys to our *Ignite Change Method*™ is focusing on the work with a select group of internal team members working with a specific group of customers. As the method implies, we're setting up a trial, but specifically working with internal partners who are outstanding at working collaboratively with a commitment to the Shared Values Framework and with complete absence of toxic behaviors.

The cross functional *TransFormation Team* is made up of a broad range of talent from across the organization, each with a proven Emergent Leaders mindset. It's this powerful combination that brings together results that are innovative and transformational in nature.

Let's examine each stage, one at a time, and see how the Ignite Change Method has been proven to be very effective to assist leaders in driving change in the *Own It Culture*.

CHAPTER 8

Own It:
Rewriting
the Ways of
Management

“

Obstacles are those frightful things you can see when you take your eyes off your goal."
– Henry Ford

As we build out an *Own It Culture*, it's important to align all our thoughts and practices. In fact, success in this undertaking typically does not work unless every part is aligned. This obviously includes how we lead and manage in the organization. I say obvious because we have just spent the majority of the book talking about it. However, I think it's important that we pause and take a look at some conventional management thinking that you may be wrestling with in your organization.

Conventional management thinking and practices utilizes one or more of three strategies intended to improve outcomes and results:

- **Impose Performance Standards:** The goal is to identify the specific actions and behaviors expected of people working within the system.
- **Set Targets:** The goal is to define the expected outcomes of individuals and groups working within the system.
- **Maximize Output:** The goal is to achieve maximum efficiency by maximizing the output of the system, and thereby reducing the cost-per-unit of a product or service.

What's wrong with these being a focus? Unfortunately, these three strategies, if not handled correctly, can directly complete against what we strive to experience in an *Own It Culture*. When not leveraged, each can cause unintended negative consequences, create stress, failure and drive away customers.

Before we examine why these three strategies fail to deliver customer values, let's look at how they came into common use.

In 1945, Peter Drucker penned *Concept of the Corporation*.[36] His famous theory, "Management by Objectives" popularized the use of mutually agreed-upon targets and performance standards as a means of boosting operational performance. Unlike Taylor, Drucker spent little time observing and writing about work on the front lines.

Instead, he focused his attention on management and management theory. While he wrote extensively about the "need for community" where the "knowledge worker's" social needs could be met, his organizational solutions were still fundamentally focused on how management could exert control over workers' activity and behavior. Albeit more subtly though than either Frederick Taylor or B. F. Skinner.

Influenced by Drucker's thinking, targets and performance standards and production targets have become the norm in the past several decades. Performance standards and targets are intended to improve the level of performance in the organization by defining desired behaviors and actions. They tell workers exactly *how* to do their jobs.

For example, workers might be required by their company's performance standards to produce products following a defined set of specifications. Similarly, distributors of a company's products might be required to follow performance standards for shelf-sets, displays and point-of-sale materials.

Targets define the specific outcomes expected of individuals and groups. Targets tell individuals exactly how much they're required to produce in a given period of time. For example, workers might be given a target to reach a specific quota each hour, day, week or month; and if they fail to meet the quota, they're at first reprimanded, and perhaps later, fired. Distributors might be required to meet certain targets or quotas of product sold in order to retain distribution rights.

Distributors often make certain they hit their supplier's targets by maximizing their system's output. For example, they will, because it's demanded of them by their supplier, place a new product at every retail outlet in their territory. They know in advance, from observing sales trends in each account, that some new products are highly unlikely to sell in certain accounts.

Later, when those products remain unsold, they must be picked up by the distributor (if required to do so) and redistributed to accounts where the product is selling or discarded. In industries where the retailer is stuck with product that won't sell, the retailer understandably becomes less inclined to do business with the distributor in the future.

The problem with performance standards and targets is that they ignore three important facts that Deming taught and that other systems thinkers confirm:

1. Customer demand is highly variable.

2. Any system's outputs are also variable.

3. Since management designs the systems, workers have little control over how well the systems work and little or no responsibility for improving them.

Therefore, achieving targets, quotas and performance standards is often not within the control of the people trying their best to adhere to them. This, therefore, unintentionally encourages them to try to avoid responsibility and accountability.

From a motivational viewpoint, when people fail to hit a target, performance standard or quota, they tend to feel guilty, ashamed and responsible. Consequently, targets, performance standards and quotas often destroy worker motivation and morale and teach them "learned helplessness."

When morale drops, the typical team member's energy is directed toward surviving rather than on improving individual performance or improving the performance of the organization. These are the very things targets, performance standards, and quotas are designed to enhance!

The main problem with quotas, targets and performance standards is that they're based on what the ownership or management hopes their organization will produce, usually an increase over the previous year. Of course, management can rarely anticipate changes in the economy or the market, which might impact customer demand.

They most often tend to ignore the variability of output caused by the design of the system itself. If the targets or quotas aren't reached, the blame is placed on the people working in the system. The conclusion is that the team members they've hired aren't sufficiently motivated.

One solution to the motivation problem frequently employed in conventional management systems is to turn up the pressure on team members, or simply replace team members who fail to produce. Of course, finding team members who can produce in a high-stakes environment is easier said than done. Another strategy to increase motivation is to find a tougher, more authoritarian manager or supervisor who is willing to push employees to work harder and longer. It's not surprising that in these high-stakes, target-driven cultures, team members and managers come and go frequently.

Performance Standard Consequences

Adopting performance standards, while intended to improve quality, can actually produce some unintended consequences, like forcing customers to accept services and products – whether they want them that way or not.

The problem is that customers don't always want things the way they've been designed or produced. Customers are notorious for wanting things *their way*. More importantly, performance standards impede the ability of team members to respond to variation in customer demand. In effect, team members are forced to choose between responding to a customer's request that is outside of the performance standards (risking punishment) or conforming to the performance standard (risking alienation of the customer).

Suppose a customer has purchased a new phone from a local retailer. The customer takes it home, opens the package, and begins reading the owner's manual. As they read carefully, it becomes evident that the phone they purchased has inadequate storage space for their music, movie and photo collection. They decide they want to upgrade to a phone with more memory, so they set it aside until they have time to return to the store.

Returning to the store eight days later, they approach a customer service rep and explain why they would like to exchange the phone. The service rep is conflicted. The performance standard states that they can make an exchange on products only when they're returned within seven days (unless approved by a store manager), and only if the seal on the original packaging is undisturbed (the packaging seal has been broken).

Now the rep faces a dilemma. Because they're alone in the store and can't ask their manager for permission to make the exchange, they risk alienating the customer by sticking to the performance standard, or risk upsetting their manager by making the exchange. In most cases, the rep will stick to the performance standard and send the customer home, unhappy.

Performance standards, no matter how well intended, tend to inhibit the ability of people working within the system to deliver products and services tailored to the needs of each customer. More often than not, an unhappy customer will simply choose to do business elsewhere in the future.

Targets Tension

Targets are a commonly used tool to define expected outcomes for individuals and teams. While people are working hard to reach their targets, they often ignore the unintended negative consequences.

Let's look at the conventional management assumptions behind using targets and why these assumptions are flawed.

The problem is that while team members work hard to hit their targets and earn their bonuses, their communications became overly optimistic about growth. In other words, under pressure to hit targets, people resort to telling management what they wanted to hear. They may not intend to lie, but in the end, their "overly optimistic reports" prove to be untrue.

Too often, targets represent something management hopes the organization can accomplish. The problem is that there are frequently a number of factors well outside the organization's control, such as the economic, social or political environment, the weather, or even poor judgment.

Then there is the challenge of involving team members in setting targets. Although we could view this as creating greater engagement, leaders often find that an unintended consequence is setting up a competitive environment. This competitive environment encouraged them to make projections that ultimately over-promised and under-delivered.

Maximizing Output Creates Waste

The primary purpose of maximizing output is to bring cost down and keeping the cost of production low is a perfectly reasonable goal. But the first problem with trying to continually maximize output is that this strategy ignores the fact that no matter how well a system is designed, or the expertise of the talent you have working the system, output always varies because of circumstances and demand.

One of the greatest challenges when working to maximize output is what I call the "exponential growth of stress, failures and waste." I am referring to the phenomenon that occurs when any system is pushed to the limit of its capacity.

When work volume is near normal, the waste in the system's design remains hidden. The problem occurs when demand on the system increases, and the system's ability to deal with *normal* levels of pressure begin to break down. As the pressure on the system grows, the amount of time to complete activities increases dramatically and the amount of stress, failures and waste swells.

As I like to say, "Add pressure to any environment, whether people or process, and you will quickly begin to see the cracks." Understandably, when cracks show, customers typically aren't very unhappy, team members feel helpless and results suffer.

Measurements that Matter

If our goal when building the *Own It Culture* is to bring things into alignment, how do we address setting performance standards, designing targets, and maximizing outputs? For leaders, this comes down to measuring what matters and keeping in mind that what matters is the team's ability to respond to the customer.

John Seddon, a leading contemporary systems thinker, describes customers this way: "Customers make customer-shaped demands; if the systems cannot absorb this variety, costs will rise."[37]

That cost is not just monetary, but potentially the variable demands can lead to significant organizational disruption, team member fatigue and frustration, and ultimately disengagement on the part of internal team members and customers.

What Seddon is saying is that this customer-adaptive capability must be designed into the way we do the work. This is accomplished by asking the people who work in the system every day (not managers or supervisors) to become responsible for designing the work processes, monitoring quality, and continually improving the ability to respond to what customers need and want.

I referenced *Systems Thinking* earlier when taking about assembling the right resources, or tools, to assist the team in getting the work done. *System Thinking* recognizes the relationship between *Purpose* (what the organization does – in our work we refer to this as the 'Why'), *Measures* (knowing how well the organization is performing) and *Method* (exactly how the organization does it – we refer to this as the 'Way').

As leaders building an *Own It Culture*, we must learn to take a bigger and broader view. You can see the challenges caused by the current organizational design, the opportunities for improvement and the means to realize them. Taking this broader view always provides a compelling case for change, and challenges leaders to see the value of designing and managing work in a different way. The *Own It* approach is to design for customer demand, (the things customers want to see from you).

Own It Cultures apply three measurement criteria:

1. Measure only those things that relate to what customers value.

2. Design measures that help team members understand the system and improve the ability to deliver customer value.

3. Make sure that the people responsible for doing the work are doing the measuring.

In conventional cultures, managers and supervisors are in charge of measuring their work group's results and the individual contributions of each member of the group (through annual performance reviews and other review processes.) In an *Own It Culture*, however, people on the frontlines do most of the measuring using the *Own It Culture Measurement Criteria*.

Measure What is Valued

Team members measure only those things that relate to what their customers value. For example, at a fast-food restaurant, customers value speed and low cost the most; presentation and quality are secondary. In fast food restaurants that have established an *Own It Culture*, they create a system that will deliver what customers want from fast food restaurants: inexpensive food delivered quickly.

They realize, of course, that in addition to speed and low cost, their customers also value presentation and quality, so they add playgrounds for the kids, comfortable and bright areas, as well as clean restrooms.

In up-scale restaurants, however, presentation and quality are what customers value most. So, in upscale restaurants that have established an *Own It Culture*, they create a system that shouts high quality from the moment their guests drive up. This might include valet parking; and a maître d' dressed formally and addressing patrons as "Sir" and "Madam."

The waiters probably wear black slacks or skirts, crisply starched white shirts, pressed aprons, and hair that is neatly groomed. Tables are most likely set with linen cloths, crystal-clear water goblets and wine glasses, and gleaming cutlery. The entire dining experience is designed to appeal to the senses. Whatever is valued, should be measured. So, whether it's speed, quality, ambience or the feel, measure those things because that is what matters to the customer most of all.

Measure to Improve Delivery

Team members design measures that help them understand and improve the system's ability to deliver customer value. Would fast-food and gourmet restaurants measure the same things? Yes and no. Because they're both in the restaurant business, there would be some things they both would measure, such as the amount spent per ticket and which items on the menu sell more.

The difference is that the fast-food restaurant would be very interested in measuring how long it takes to complete an order — with the goal of reducing the time customers have to wait. After all, customers choose fast-food restaurants because they want their food fast. On the other hand, the gourmet restaurant might be more interested in carefully monitoring every aspect of presentation: the ambiance of the dining room, the precise manners of the waiter, wine steward, server and table-busser, and how the food looks on the plate.

To reiterate, each type of restaurant designs their food delivery system to provide more of what their customers value, and the members of each self-managing team closely monitor how well their system delivers those things.

Team Members Own the Measuring

The people who are doing the work do the measuring. In conventional cultures, the measuring is done either by a supervisor and/or an auditor. As I explained earlier, this is based on the assumption that people's behavior and activity are the main issue, not the system design or the measurements themselves.

People in an *Own It Culture* make a different assumption: problems are usually the result of the design of the system, not the people working within the system. This creates a level of accountability on the frontlines that is not possible in an authoritarian culture.

Put simply, when people become stewards of the measurement systems, they're eager to step up and become stewards of the systems by continuously making sure that the systems are designed to respond to what customers want.

CHAPTER 9

Own It:
Expecting
Everyone to Play

"

Success is the sum of small efforts, repeated day-in, and day-out."
– Robert Collier

The foundation principles discussed throughout this book are built on engagement and empowerment. The *Own It Culture* will only be fully experienced when people, each and every team member, is willing to take ownership for the work, take responsibility of for how they're showing up, and ultimately take actions that make a difference.

In conventional organizations, managers spend most of their time "thinking," while front-line workers spend most of their time "doing." Thinking typically includes experimenting with changes to the organizational structure, the systems and processes. They also have the responsibility of directing the activity of those who report to them. Managers are the problem-solvers, using their creativity to find solution to issues, particularly those that aren't addressed by the organizations policies and procedures.

Managers set the priorities. They decide what work is important and in what order it should be performed. They set the policies both for what team members are expected to do and for how to deal with customers. Managers are also responsible for developing and implementing operational plans. This includes everything from annual budgets to introducing new products and services.

Managers bear the burden of creating, maintaining and improving the systems. It's their job to identify and fix problems that occur and to make sure that the people who report to them are completing daily customer transactions. Managers also measure the results of individuals and teams, often creating charts and graphs to let their direct reports know whether they're hitting their targets and whether their activity meets the performance standards.

Contrast this with an *Own It Culture*, where the self-managing teams and *TransFormation Zones* are the norm. All of these responsibilities are put in the hands of the people doing the work, the people on the frontlines, who are closest to the systems and processes and who are closest to the customer. Leaders take on a supporting role, partnering with team members and providing coaching and an extra set of hands as needed.

Below are eight essential actions we need to foster within an *Own It Culture*. The principles and coaching we've already discussed throughout the book are designed to bring these eight actions to life in the hands of team members.

#1 - Experiment: Think Outside the Box

People in an *Own It Culture* are encouraged to explore and experiment. Encouraging experimentation carries certain risks, of course, not the least of which is *failure*. But as any scientist will tell you, today's failures are the price of future innovations. Even small incremental improvements cannot occur without a willingness to risk failure.

In fact, failure is expected and even celebrated because people understand that each failure provides an opportunity to learn and is a step closer to success.

In order to make experimentation the norm, people must have the authority to make day-to-day decisions. They must be responsible for experimenting with the design and maintenance of the systems they work in.

By doing this, they become responsible for planning and executing *boost experiments* every day. Boost experiments, as you may recall, are proposed changes to the system, structured as small projects or experiments. They're designed to test the effect of modifications to systems and processes before making them permanent.

Team members keep a careful log of boost experiments and their effects. The log lists problems observed, the countermeasures for each problem, the effect of the change, and the team members reactions to the countermeasures. In an *Own It Culture*, team members are expected to experiment as frequently as possible.

#2 - Be Self-Directed: Get in the Driver's Seat

People in an *Own It Culture* have the freedom to choose their own job responsibilities. This doesn't mean that people have the power to choose not to do unpleasant or difficult tasks. Rather, it means they've accepted the responsibility for choosing to do these tasks and to be accountable for the results.

It's the element of choice that is important. When people feel they're being coerced into doing unpleasant or difficult tasks, they're much more likely to either do the job poorly or not at all. On the other hand, when people are given the freedom to choose to take on difficult or unpleasant tasks, they're much more likely to do their best.

Whether the tasks are effortless and fun, or challenging or distasteful, people should have the freedom to make decisions each day about what they'll do and how they'll do it. They should also have the freedom to design the systems they work in and be responsible for making improvements to workflow. They should have the freedom to do whatever is needed in order to satisfy their customers.

Senior leaders in an *Own It Culture* understand and have accepted the fact that no one knows the systems and customers better than the people closest to the work. Because of this, it only makes sense to them that self-directed people should take on the responsibility for designing and improving the systems. The goal is to help every individual learn to become self-directed.

Of course, this doesn't happen overnight. For individuals to become self-directed (empowered), they need to have mastered important skills, to be committed to their jobs and to have passion for their work.

As James A. Autry and Stephen Mitchell write, "Real empowerment is not about taking power from the top and spreading it through the company. On the contrary, it is about you as a manager recognizing that your employees already have power. It's the power of their skills, their commitment to the job, and their passion for the work. This is not your power to give. Real power is power that you can recognize and honor by creating an environment in which the power can be expressed for the good of all. It's power *with* your people, not power *over* your people. In the same way, your own power comes not from your authority. It comes from your abilities, experience, and commitment. The real job of empowerment is bringing the power of your employees together with your own power in order to produce the best results for everyone."[38]

#3 - Be Creative: The Curious & Courageous

Creativity establishes a high level of engagement and commitment at all levels of an organization. Creativity goes well beyond the artistic: it means being imaginative, enthusiastic and energetic. This means that people have the freedom to work independently on projects they find interesting and challenging, the essential elements of intrinsic motivation.

People design their jobs so that they have enough creativity to keep them engaged and committed to their work. When they become bored with or overwhelmed by their jobs, they take the initiative to swap responsibilities with their co-workers or to ask for help. As people experiment, they strive to be imaginative, inventive and original in their thinking. Each job includes elements of fun, energy and enthusiasm, which lead to a higher level of engagement and commitment to their work and their co-workers.

People in an *Own It Culture* must be encouraged to think "outside the box" and to try new things without needing to check for prior approval. This mode of thinking is critical in a culture where experimentation is encouraged. Rather than hearing phrases like "This is the way we do things here," or "We tried that once and it failed," or "Our policy says...," or "Our process dictates...," the members of self-managing teams are more likely to hear, "Let's give it a try and see what happens," or "That's an interesting idea, let's play with it for a while," or "I've never thought of doing things that way before. This could be interesting!"

One of the creative elements of *TransFormation Zones* is that people working in them often come become creative in direct response to changes to market conditions or changes in customer demand. Well-established conventional organizations often don't see changes in market conditions coming. Their tendency is to either anticipate a continuation of the present conditions, or to be unrealistically optimistic about the organization's future. But market changes do occur often without warning. This is when creativity is particularly important. When markets change, the old way of doing things no longer applies; a new way of operating is required. Finding a new way of operating obviously requires creativity with people coming together to find innovative new solutions to the market change.

Another creative element of the *TransFormation Zone* is that membership is very fluid; people are able to move from one *TransFormation Zone* to another depending on how their skills, experience and creativity might contribute to the success of the group. In fact, often individuals are members of more than one team at the same time. They may even play different roles in each team, sharing leadership on one group or being more of a resource to another. This fluidity, sometimes called flow, encourages co-workers to find creative solutions and celebrate success together.

Creativity has a distinctively spiritual aspect to it, connecting us to the supernatural and to each other. In their book, *Leading with Soul,* Lee Bolman and Terrence Deal quote Harvey Cox, a leading American theologian at the Harvard Divinity School:

"Man in his very essence is *homo festivus* and *homo fantasia*. Celebrating and imagining are integral parts of his humanity but the western industrial man in the past few centuries has begun to lose his capacity for festivity and fantasy. The loss is personal, social, and religious. It deprives us of a central ingredient of our lives. It makes us provincial and maladaptive. It stills our sense of connection to the cosmos, of contributing to something larger than ourselves."

Bolman and Deal go on to say that creativity is about authorship: "It's the feeling of putting your own signature on your work. It's the sheer joy of creating something of lasting value. The feeling of adding something special to the world." [39]

#4 - Set Priorities: Craft a Vision & Stick-to-it

Setting day-to-day priorities is dependent on people knowing and understanding the direction and purpose of the organization. People in an *Own It Culture* know exactly what tasks they're responsible for, and how what they do each day contributes to the success of the organization.

In other words, they can see and understand how the results they produce each day contribute to the success of their own team and their organization. Seeing and understanding this connection is what enables them to choose priorities appropriately.

People working in an *Own It Culture* have fundamental business skills to understand financial and technical data, so that they can determine their strategic and tactical priorities. Just as human beings require air and water to survive, organizations need two basic things to survive: (1) Cash Flow to fund current expenses and (2) Profit to fund capital investments for the future.

So, in an *Own It Culture*, basic financial literacy (at the very least: read and understand a Profit & Loss Statement and a Balance Sheet) becomes a requirement for membership; all members know how to construct a budget proposal. Also, members understand and are able to use technical data unique to their disciplines (for example: anything that tracks workflow issues, causes of waste, and quality output).

People working in *TransFormation Zones* understand their customer's priorities and are able to respond appropriately. In fact, they understand that in order for the organization to survive, the organization's priorities must align with the customer's priorities. While most organizations *claim* to be customer focused, few have developed systems for uncovering and responding to what customers really want.

#5 - Establish Policies: Put Up the Fences

In conventional hierarchical cultures, only boards of directors and senior executives have the authority to establish policies. Workers are expected to comply with the policies, not to challenge them. Policies are created to ensure that workers are doing what they should be doing, and to define for supervisors the specific performance issues they should be monitoring. Policies set by management also define for workers what they are and aren't allowed to do for customers.

However, in an *Own It Culture*, policies are divided into three categories: (1) *Purpose Policies*, what John and Miriam Carver call "Ends Policies"[40] set by the board, defining the reason the organization exists, (2) *Strategic Policies* set by the senior executive, defining the operating philosophy and a path toward the future, and (3) *Tactical Policies* set by members of each *TransFormation Zone*, defining how work is done and how customers are served.

Members of an *Own It Culture* understand, accept and support the board's *Purpose Policies,* which explain the reason for the organization's existence and their expectations from the senior executive team. Everyone in the organization, not just the senior executive team, should know these purpose policies. These are communicated in a variety of ways, such as in speeches made by senior executives, in written communications, and most importantly, in group discussions where members of the organization have an opportunity to ask clarifying questions.

The senior executive has the responsibility of clearly communicating their Strategic Policies, which describe their operating philosophy, establish the boundaries within which business is to be conducted, and clearly define their expectations for the workforce. Members of self-managing teams and *TransFormation Zones* have complete authority and responsibility for setting *Tactical Policies* that relate to the systems they work in.

They have this responsibility because they are the ones who must make the systems work and they have the responsibility of challenging any policy that stands in the way of being responsible and accountable to customers. Setting Tactical Policies provides team members with the ability to control workflow, solve problems, and meet the unique needs of each customer.

#6 - Create the Map: Plan the Work, Work the Plan

In conventional top-down cultures, while people down the chain of command may be asked to give their input on plans, in most cases, senior managers have already made up their minds. The process often works something like this: senior management ask for tactical plans generated at the "local" level by mid-level managers and perhaps even front-line workers. Often those at the lower levels learn quickly that they're simply "going through the motions" until senior management finally reveals their plans by demanding that the tactical plans conform to their pre-determined strategic objectives.

In stark contrast, an *Own It Culture* expects people working together in self-managing teams to develop tactical plans and to help make them successful. Rather than relying on senior executives or powerful senior staffers to develop tactical plans, members at every level of the organization are involved in planning and execution. Senior executives make their strategic goals known and then ask mid-level and frontline team members to develop plans to reach these goals. In the process, they ask for honest feedback on the workability of the strategic goals and are prepared to modify their strategic goals if necessary.

Members of self-managing teams are responsible for planning budgets, schedules, production, and delivery at the tactical level. They're also responsible for measuring results and for modifying plans when results don't match expectations. They know that no matter how well constructed, plans depend on a set of assumptions that may or may not turn out to be correct. In order for plans to be useful, they must provide for contingencies. Therefore, the rule on self-managing teams is: "Plan but be prepared to modify the plan."

The U.S. Marine Corps has adopted a planning strategy that involves soldiers of every rank. "The Marines don't distinguish between followers and potential leaders; they believe every member of the Corps must be able to lead."[41] In fact, when planning for battle, the Corps brings together a representative group of Marines from every rank, from private to colonel.

Understanding the exigencies of war, they seek input from everyone gathered to draw up not one, but three battle plans. The assumption is that in a flash of gunfire, a Marine of any rank may be called on to step forward and lead, making battlefield decisions about what plan to follow or whether, based on the circumstances, to come up with a new plan.[42]

#7 - Remove Blocks: Bust Down the Barriers

People working together in an *Own It Culture* identify the causes of *TransFormation Blocks* and for reducing or eliminating them.

TransFormation Blocks are anything that inhibits the customer transaction, disappoints the customer, slows the process, or causes other types of waste within the system.

Having the authority to remove *TransFormation Blocks* has tremendous benefits for team members and even more benefits for the organization and for customers. For team members, *TransFormation Blocks* tend to make life more difficult. Therefore, removing *TransFormation Blocks* and improving workflow means getting rid of things that make work life hard to bear, such as over-processing, waiting, excess motion, and any other kind of defect that may occur within the system which makes the job less pleasant and more likely to cause physical injury.

Removing *TransFormation Blocks* and improving workflow adds to the sense of empowerment for people on the frontlines and gives them a greater sense of control over their daily lives.

Removing *TransFormation Blocks* and improving workflow have obvious benefits for the organization, such as less waste and unnecessary cost, and of course, delivers real benefits for customers in faster service and better products. Typically, says systems expert, John Seddon, most of the calls coming into a service desk are the result of a company failing to do something correctly for a customer the first time.

Giving team members the authority to look into the causes of these failures and giving them the power to initiate corrective improvements to the workflow dramatically decreases the number of failures and frustrations. The result is better quality for customers and stronger financial and impact results for the company.

#8 - Drive Impact: From Transactions to TransFormation

Having the authority to complete transactions, without handing them off, helps people at every level of the organization develop a sense of ownership. People in an *Own It Culture* make every effort to own and complete transactions, rather than handing them off to a co-worker or supervisor.

This approach gives team members the ability to respond to special requests by customers and allows the transaction to be completed faster and with more customer value. By completing customer transactions, members are responsible for delivering what customers expect – no more, no less.

Much has been written in recent years about exceeding customer expectations – which seems like a good idea. However, experience has taught organizations that have tried to make exceeding customer expectations an operating principle, that while many customers may be delighted that they're getting more than they asked for, it turns out that some customers are not delighted. In fact, they're unhappy that they didn't get exactly what they asked for. To those customers, too much of a good thing is not a good thing.

Even for those customers who are surprised and delighted the first or second time the organization exceeds their expectations, it's highly likely that at some time, the customer's expectations may begin to outpace the organization's ability to deliver. This means that even though you've delivered what you promised, you still have a disappointed customer. Therefore, it becomes everyone's responsibility to complete transactions and deliver customer value in a way that your competition can't or won't.

James Belasco and Ralph Stayer, authors of the best-selling book *Flight of the Buffalo* write, "Maintaining long-term customers is about creating value – doing something customers want different or better than anybody else. Customers are where it all begins. Delighting them. Talking to them in their language. Selling them what they want. Learning from them what they need. Most of all, getting and keeping customers is about everyone in the organization owning the responsibility to get and keep customers. Every person, every day, views every activity, every procedure, every process, through the perspective of 'What is great performance for my customer?' Each and every person owns the responsibility for delighting customers. That's the right and only focus."[43]

In other words, both the customer and the organization benefit when self-managing team members have the authority to complete transactions in a way that delights customers and lead to a truly transformational experience.

Coaching Corner

Every individual, and the teams they're part of, are encouraged to engage in *Own It Actions.* These actions that are usually reserved for managers and supervisors in conventional environments become the responsibility of self-managing individuals and teams.

To assess how much your organization encourages people to take responsibility, complete *The Own It Action Assessment* found on the resources page of our website.

Visit www.own-it-the-book.com/resources for more information.

Final Thoughts

"

*Don't be afraid to give up
the good to go for the great."*
– John D. Rockefeller

Deciding to establish an *Own It Culture* by changing the social contract, encouraging Emergent Leaders and delivering customer value, can yield incredible improvements in operational results, in team member satisfaction and engagement, and particularly in the ability to deliver customer value. But make no mistake. Making this transformation requires a great deal of *courage* on the part of leaders to insist that every member of the organization be both responsible and accountable.

It also takes a great deal of courage on the part of team members to give up their learned helplessness or toxic behaviors and step up to be responsible and accountable. Breaking down the walls of old behaviors, obsolete management models, and ending adversarial relationships between management and labor is not easy. It takes an incredible amount of patience and persistence. The rewards (helping your organization succeed in a challenging world) are well worth the price.

One thing our work has taught us over the years, is that transforming a culture is challenging. As I meet with leaders at the start of the journey, I share with them some of the realities of the path they're about to undertake.

It's common to see a 40% change over in your team members and anywhere from an 18-month to three-year process to drive the change. To put it bluntly, it's not for the faint of heart. Values will be challenged and redefined. Long-standing practices will be thrown out and rebuilt. Every member of the organization will be asked to work differently. Just like changing your personal health habits, every action you take, attitude you adjust or new practice you implement is designed to bring an *Own It Culture* to life from the core.

It's my hope that the information we've walked through in this book has (at the very least) inspired you to want to *Own It*. Let me put on my coaching hat for a moment. This transformational work is hard work. Don't try to accomplish things on your own. Let me encourage you to take a few action items:

1. Check out this book's website. It's full of valuable resources to help you through the process. Take the *Own It* assessments. As a valued reader, these assessments are completely free and will give you tremendous insights to guide your steps.

2. Sign up for our online newsletter and blog. Each communication we put together is designed to spark your leadership.

3. Consider a Culture Survey. When you're ready, the data and feedback you get from a comprehensive survey process will be invaluable. Whether working with our team or another consulting group, the insights you will gain and the action plans you undertake will be game changers.

4. Check out our book series **Would You Work for You?** This four-part book series will challenge your leadership and continue to bring to life the concepts and actions for building an *Own It Culture*. I have included some more information on the series at the end of this book.

5. Reach out. At the end of the day, I'm in a relationship business and what makes the work of writing books or doing podcasts worth it is when I get to connect with my readers. I've included all my contact information at the end of the book. Your story is important to me. Your work is important to me. Don't be a stranger.

Get Up. Show Up. Fire Up. Own It!
All the best,
Chris

Acknowledgments

I'd like to thank the people who have significantly influenced my life, my thinking, and my personal growth: my parents and first mentors, Jim and Ona Mae Ihrig, and my wife and best friend, Kris Ihrig.

As the youngest of six, I want to thank each of my siblings for holding me down for my own good, picking me up when needed and training mom and dad so I could get away with things.

To my own kids, Emily, Gabe, Anna and Alec, as your dad, I've learned so much from each of you, whether it was perceived as a good day or one of the more challenging ones. You have shown me how much work life and family life mirror each other as we have tried to make life work. I'd also like to acknowledge the profound influence of the faith and not-for-profit communities I have been a part of throughout my life. I've encountered so many people who, in choosing to serve others, help to create an *Own It Culture.*

A special acknowledgment goes out to my colleague, Randy Spitzer. Randy is truly a generous leader who has brought the *Own It Attitude* to life in all that he does. Without his significant contributions and investment, this book would not exist.

Most of the ideas presented in this book are not mine alone; many were born from deep conversations; the work of creative and talented authors and researchers. Others are the fruit of much thought and discussion between leaders and me, and, of course, some are my own creation. Over the last many years, the team at *Fired Up! Culture* has tested these ideas with the help of our clients who share our passion for creating an *Own It Culture.*

With sincere gratitude,
Chris

Additional Resources

Although we do consider *Own It* to be an important resource full of meaningful thoughts and resources, the reality is it can only scratch the surface. Becoming a *Culture Champion* and building an amazing workplace takes time, effort and dedication.

Leading yourself well is a lifelong journey, full of daily decisions, attitude check-ins, conversations, failures and growth. For continually updated resources, visit *www.firedupculture.com/resources*.

The different assessments referenced in this book provide an important resource for assisting you and the people in your organization to understand more clearly who you are and what behaviors/attitudes you're bringing to the workplace. They will give you the opportunity to identify your personal gaps as you strive to "lead yourself well" and will give you a clear path forward.

Each of these assessments are designed to be taken online and will require only a few minutes of your time. There is no cost to complete the *Own It Assessments* listed. However, we will ask you to register so we can continue to grow our relationship with you.

Own It! Assessments

- The Own It! – Responsibility Inhibiting Behaviors (RIB) Self-Assessment™
- The Emergent Leader Self-Assessment™
- The Own It! – Action Assessment™

Organizational Culture & Additional Leadership Assessments

- Fired Up Culture Index™
- Fired Up Culture Leadership360™

More Books from Fired Up Publishing

Fired Up! Brands is deeply dedicated to building exceptional resources to assist you, your team and your organization. Along with *Own It!*, we've developed a book series to assist you with your leadership journey.

Our series **Would You Work for You**, which I wrote with Dr. Tim Yeomans, is available from a variety of resources including our websites (above) and by visiting *www.wouldyouworkforyou.com* and on Amazon.

As a current friend of the firm, you can receive the best prices and personal service by simply visiting www.firedupculture.com/resources.

Whether you're looking for one book or purchasing in bulk for your team, our specialized care team are on hand to help you. As a special limited time offer, use the code **OWNIT15** for a 15% discount on your next order.

About the Author – Chris J. Ihrig

A Note from Chris:

I'm a blessed man. I didn't get what I thought I wanted when I began my college journey as an art student to be a world-class photographer. What I got instead has been a winding road of a career: first as a recreational therapist working with clients with Traumatic Brain Injuries, then becoming a Director, running a community program for high-risk disabled adults, then leading several retirement communities, running the operations of a community homeless shelter. Then I made a big move to being a senior team member in Human Resources at World Vision, and for the last several decades, I tried to sell the outrageous idea that in the right working environment, ordinary people can and will do the most extraordinary things for their organizations and for their customers.

During each curve and stop along the career journey, I attempted to learn something about myself first, the people I worked with second and observe what made organizations run. What I have come to realize is Workplace Culture makes a difference. If you get it right, people's lives are changed and our communities are positively impacted.

About Chris

Chris was born and raised in Seattle, Washington. He attained a BA from The Evergreen State College and an MBA in Organizational Development from Regent University. He currently lives in the Pacific

Northwest with his wife of 33 years, Kris. He and his wife are very proud parents of four adult children and their growing extended family.

In his free time, Chris enjoys playing golf, watching baseball as well as studying history and technology. His great passion is his 1982 Jaguar XJS car and he enjoys driving it every time he gets behind the wheel. When he gets the chance, he enjoys traveling, immersing himself in different cultures, connecting with people and nature, and sampling food from around the world.

Chris has been recognized nationally as an authority in the fields of Leadership Development, Organizational Change and Culture. Chris is an internationally recognized speaker and author. He has completed several other writing projects, including the **Would You Work for You Series** which he wrote with his longtime friend and colleague, Dr. Tim Yeomans.

You can contact Chris on:

LinkedIn: *https://www.linkedin.com/in/chrisihrig/*

Twitter: *@chrisihrig*

Email: *cihrig@firedupculture.com*

About Our Firm – Fired Up Culture

Fired-Up! Culture is a worldwide consulting, training and coaching firm with corporate headquarters in the Pacific Northwest of the United States. Over the past few decades, our team has partnered with organizations and leaders around the globe to build business cultures that engage people and achieve breakthrough results.

Fired-Up! Culture's mission is to equip and build leadership capacity through talent management-focused consulting services that provide relevant and timely resources for our clients. Fired-Up's commitment to excellence supports a focused and intentional investment in the people and systems of these organizations to achieve breakthrough results.

Our leadership development and change management processes are used by a diverse client base around the world. We've had the privilege of shaping the philosophies, practices and skills of thousands of dynamic leaders, managers and teams. Our tools have been successfully used and implemented by hundreds of organizations and their team members.

Our coaching, consulting and facilitation services provide the focus and insight needed to drive lasting change.

For more information about Fired Up!, please visit:

Website: *www.firedupculture.com*

Glossary

Accountabilities - results that an individual or group has agreed to or promised to deliver to customers, colleagues, and the organization (see also: *Responsibilities*).

Application Meetings - an opportunity for all members of the organization to gather together in small groups to talk about how the organization is progressing toward an *Own It Culture*.

Boost Initiative - methodology for studying real-life organizational issues or series of issues that, if properly addressed, resolved, or enhanced, would benefit the work team, the organization and the customers.

Bullying Behavior - any action used to control the behavior of others, such as verbally attacking, keeping score, finding fault, needing to be right, or refusing to forgive, creating diversions, playing the victim, avoiding, and giving up

Coach - the first of the five actions of an *Emergent Leader:* helping co-workers develop the knowledge and skills they need to do their jobs (see also: *Emergent Leaders).*

Connect People to Resources - the third of the five actions of an Emergent Leader: helping co-workers learn how to find and access additional resources they might need to meet new challenges (see also: *Emergent Leaders* and *Resources).* Resources include:

- Information: made available to anyone in the organization who needs it; information is as transparent as possible without violating confidences.

- Time: found by removing waste, improving workflow, reordering priorities or negotiating with co-workers.
- Money: making a business case for additional funds needed to complete a project or improve the system.
- Workforce: making the case for adding people to a project, work group or system.

Customer Value - anything and everything that customers value and they are willing to pay a premium for. Creating customer values asks three primary questions:

1. What's the best way for us to organize to convenience our customers, rather than merely to convenience ourselves?

2. How can we make it easy for our customers to do business with us?

3. How do we ensure that our *Self-Managing Teams* and individual members have both responsibility and accountability for removing *TransFormation Blocks* from the workflow and for delivering value to our customers?

Deputy Fife Syndrome - asserting control or authority in an inappropriate or destructive manner as a bully.

Emergent Leader - an individual who steps forward to lead at the precise moment the team can benefit from their leadership skills and/or experience using one or more of the following leadership actions:

- Coach: helping co-workers develop the knowledge and skills they need to do their jobs.
- Offer Counsel: helping co-workers to learn how to solve everyday issues and problems.
- Connect People to Resources: helping co-workers learn how to find and access the resources they might need to meet new

challenges.

- Encourage Stewardship: encouraging co-workers to take complete ownership for their jobs and systems.
- See the Big Picture: helping everyone understand how each job supports the larger purpose of the organization.

The Emergent Leader Coaching Guidelines

Guidelines for Coaching:

1. Look for a teachable moment before offering to coach.
2. Ask for permission before beginning to coach.
3. Offer coaching as a colleague, not as a superior.
4. Be willing to coach anyone who asks for help.

Guidelines for Being Coached:

1. Ask for coaching whenever you need help.
2. Be open to coaching from anyone who offers to help without becoming defensive.
3. Listen to and act on coaching tips with a "growth mindset" (a willingness to learn).
4. Give your coach feedback by asking clarifying questions.

Encourage Stewardship - the fourth of the five actions of an Emergent Leader: creating an environment where team members are able to take complete ownership for their individual jobs and for the systems (see also: *Emergent Leader*).

Fired Up Culture Index™ - one of the most comprehensive measures of corporate cultures available in the world today. It measures the values gap and employee engagement and compares the health of your organization's culture to organizations all over the world. The study has confirmed a strong correlation between the health of the organization's culture and operational results. Therefore, your organization's results are a strong predictor of your organization's future success.

Intrinsic Motivation - "being motivated by the reward of the activity itself" originally defined by psychologist Harry Harlow, PhD (1906-1981).

Leadership Coalition - senior, mid-level and frontline leaders who, together, create a compelling case for change, communicate effectively, overcome obstacles and roadblocks, create a sense of real progress, and help make the *Own It Culture* stick.

Learned Helplessness - a syndrome of passivity, dependency, and depression brought on by a loss of personal identity when individuals are subjected to arbitrary continual control of their behavior. These behaviors include being passive-aggressive, creating diversions, playing the victim, avoiding, and giving up.

More and Less Coaching Model

1. Recognize a teachable moment.
2. Empathize with the learner.
3. Make an offer to coach.
4. Coach

   o I suggest *more* of...
   o I suggest *less* of...

5. Check with the learner on the effectiveness of the coaching points.

Offer Counsel - the second of the five actions of an Emergent Leader: helping co-workers to learn how to solve problems independently (see also: *Emergent Leader).*

Pilot Projects - proposed changes to the system structured as small experiments. They are designed to test the effect of modifications to systems and processes before making them permanent.

Ignite Change Method™

- DISCOVER: study the system from end to end, looking for causes of variation.
- DREAM: identify opportunities to remove waste and improve workflow.
- DESIGN: plan and execute a series of pilot experiments.
- DELIVER: measure the results of the pilot experiments.

Responsibilities - tasks, duties, jobs, and activities belonging to an individual or group (see also: *Accountability* and *Responsibility-Taking Actions*).

Own It Actions

- **Experiment:** conducting daily nested experiments intended to make incremental improvements in the systems you work in.
- **Be Self-Directed:** owning your job without the need for supervision or external audits.
- **Be Creative:** using your creativity, imagination, enthusiasm and energy to improve workflow, remove waste and deliver solutions.
- **Set Priorities:** having the authority to own your day-to-day priorities.
- **Establish Policies:** having the authority to establish tactical policies which define how work is done and how your customers are served.

- **Plan:** having the authority and responsibility for making and modifying plans for your own work.
- **Remove *TransFormation Blocks*:** having the authority, responsibility and accountability for making meaningful changes and improvements to the systems and processes you work in.
- **Drive Impact:** having the authority, responsibility and accountability for making *TransFormation* happen and delivering solutions for customers.

See the Big Picture - the fifth of the five actions of an Emergent Leader: helping others in the organization see how what they're doing supports the larger purpose of the organization. By seeing the big picture, self-directed workers have the information they need to take full ownership of the systems they work in and for delivering solutions for customers (see also: *Emergent Leader*).

Self-Managing Teams - teams of people who take responsibility for designing systems capable of responding to the unique needs of their customers. People working together in Self-Managing Teams fix workflow problems, increase or decrease production to match customer demand, and customize products and services specifically to meet the needs of each of their unique customers.

Shared Values (The Shared Values Framework™)

- Truth — Sharing the truth with everyone.
- Trust — Trusting your co-workers and being trustworthy.
- Respect — Admiring people for their abilities, qualities, or achievements.
- Mentoring — Being open to mentoring from anyone.
- Openness — Being receptive to new ideas regardless of their source.

- Courage   Taking personal risk for the organization's sake.
- Giving Credit   Recognizing the contributions of co-workers.
- Honesty   Being honest and ethical in all matters.
- Selflessness   Putting the interests of others before your own.

Systems Thinking - a framework that's based on the belief that the only way to fully understand why problems in any system persist is to understand the *part* in relation to the *whole*. Systems Thinking asserts that the conventional approach of focusing on solving individual problems without understanding how the design of the system causes or contributes to these problems, will often exacerbate them. This is based on the belief that the component parts of a system will act differently when the system's relationships are removed and each part is viewed in isolation. In short, Systems Thinking studies the linkages and interactions between the elements that comprise the entirety of the system.

Systems Thinking Measurement Criteria

- What: measure only those things that relate to what customers value.
- How: design measures that help workers understand the system and improve your ability to deliver customer value.
- Who: make sure that the people responsible for doing the work are doing the measuring.

Teachable Moment - that moment when you're ready to be receptive to coaching and ready to hear and act on the information and direction a coach can provide.

Three-Stage Counseling Model

1. Inquiry Stage

   a) Open-Ended Questions

   b) Restating

2. Counseling Stage

   c) Observations

   d) Counseling

3. Debriefing Stage

   e) Next Steps

   f) Counseling Feedback

TransFormation Blocks - anything that inhibits a transaction, disappoints the customer, slows the process, or causes other types of waste within the system; anything that impedes the organization's ability to respond to changes in what customers want.

TransFormation Teams - small teams of people use the Pilot Project *Model* to improve workflow, remove *TransFormation Blocks* and deliver better customer value.

TransFormation Zones - cross-functional teams where customers take control of the transaction; they're organized to make it easy for customers to do business with the organization and expect team members to take responsibility for removing *TransFormation Blocks* and improving workflow.

Values Gap - the interpersonal conflict that results when there is a gap between what people expect regarding the Connected Values and what they actually observe from their managers and co-workers.

End Notes

1. A.D. Amar, Carsten Hentrich and Vlatka Hlupic, "To Be a Better Leader, Give Up Authority," *Harvard Business Review* (December 2009).

2. Edwin H. Friedman, *A Failure of Nerve: Leadership in the Age of the Quick Fix* (Seabury Books, 2007).

3. Carol S. Dweck, Ph.D., *Mindset: The New Psychology of Success* (Ballantine Books, 2007).

4. Philip Zimbardo, *The Lucifer Effect: Understanding How Good People Turn Evil* (New York: Random House, 2008).

5. Russell W. Gough, *Character is Destiny: The Value of Personal Ethics in Everyday Life* (Living Book Press, 2020).

6. Max DePree, *Leadership is an Art* (Currency, Reprint addition, 2004).

7. Robert J. Sternberg, *Successful Intelligence: How Practical and Creative Intelligence Determine Success in Life* (Plume Publishing, 1996).

8. Rosamund Stone Zander and Benjamin Zander, *The Art of Possibility* (New York: Penguin Publishing Group, 2002).

9. B. F. Skinner, *Science and Human Behavior* (New York: Macmillan Publishers, 1965).

10. Alfie Kohn, *Punished by Rewards: The Trouble with Gold Stars, Incentive Plans, A's Praise, and Other Bribes* (Mariner Books, 1999).

11. Daniel H. Pink, *Drive – The Surprising Truth About What Motivates Us,* (Reverhead Books, Penguin Group 2011).

12. Niccolo Machiavelli, *The Prince,* Second Edition (1469-1527), (Independently published, 2019).

13. Inspired by "Eliminating Your Bad Spirit" from Phillip McGraw's book, *Relationship Rescue,* (New York: Hyperion Books, 2000) and Philip Zimbardo's definition of "learned helplessness" from his book, *The Lucifer Effect* (New York: Random House, 2007).

14. Douglas Stone, Bruce Patton and Sheila Heen, *Difficult Conversations: How to Discuss What Matters Most* (Penguin Books, 2010).

15. Philip Zimbardo, *The Lucifer Effect.*

16. Ricardo Semler, *The Seven-Day Weekend: Changing the Way Work Works,* (Penguin Books Ltd, 2004).

17. Yvon Chouinard, *Let My People Go Surfing: The Education of a Reluctant Businessman* (New York, Penguin Books, 2016).

18. Frederick Taylor, *The Principles of Scientific Management* (Martino Fine Books, 2014).

19. Dennis Bakke*, Joy at Work.*

20. Jeffrey K. Liker, *The Toyota Way: 14 Management Principles from the World's Greatest Manufacturer* (New York: McGraw-Hill, 2020).

21. Dan Malachowski, "Wasted Time at Work Costing Companies Billions" (*Salary.com*, 2005).

22. Tom Peters, *The Leadership Alliance* (Video Publishing House, Inc., 1988).

23. Robert Spector, *The Nordstrom Way to Customer Experience Excellence: Creating a Values-Driven Service Culture* (New York: John Wiley & Sons, Inc., 2017).

24. Peter Block, Stewardship*: Choosing Service over Self-Interest* (San Francisco: Berrett-Koehler, 2013).

25. Ricardo Semler, *The Seven-Day Weekend.*

26. Tom Coens and Mary Jenkins, *Abolishing Performance Appraisals: Why They Backfire and What to Do Instead* (San Francisco: Berrett-Koehler Publishers, 2002).

27. Jon R. Katzenbach and Douglas K. Smith, *The Wisdom of Teams: Creating the High-Performance Organization* Harper-Collins Books, 2005).

28. Ralph Stayer, "How I Learned to Let My Workers Lead," *Harvard Business Review,* November-December 1990.

29. Patricia McLagan & Christo Nel, *The Age of Participation—New Governance for the Workplace and the World* (San Francisco: Berrett-Koehler, 1995).

30. Nathaniel Branden, Ph.D., *Taking Responsibility: Self-Reliance and the Accountable Life* (Fireside Books, 1996).

31. Robert Spector, *The Nordstrom Way*

32. Rich Teerlink, "Harley's Leadership U-Turn," *Harvard Business Review* (July-August 2000).

33. Dennis Bakke, *Joy at Work: A Revolutionary Approach to Fun on the Job (Seattle: PVG Publishers, 2005.*

34. Ricardo Semler, *The Seven-Day Weekend.*

35. Disney Institute, *Be Our Guest: Perfecting the Art of Customer Service* (Disney Enterprises, Inc., 2011).

36. Peter Drucker, *Concept of the Corporation* (Routledge, 2017).

37. John Seddon, *Freedom from Command & Control.*

38. James A. Autry and Stephen Mitchell, *Real Power: Business Lessons from the Tao Te Ching* (New York: Riverhead Books, 1998).

39. Lee G. Bolman & Terrence E. Deal, *Leading with Soul* (San Francisco: Jossey-Bass Inc., 2011).

40. John Carver and Miriam Mayhew Carver, *Reinventing Your Board: A Step-by-Step Guide to Implementing Policy Governance* (San Francisco: Jossey-Bass, John Wiley & Sons, Inc., 1997).

41. Jon R. Katzenbach and Jason A. Santamaria, "Firing up the Front Line," *Harvard Business Review,* May–June 1999.

42. Jon R. Katzenbach and Jason A. Santamaria, *The Wisdom of Teams* (Harvard Business Review Press, 2015)

43. James A. Belasco & Ralph C. Stayer, *Flight of the Buffalo* (Grand Central Publishing, 2008).

Index